Inner City Regeneration: The Demise of Regional and Local Government

Studies in Law and Politics

Published by Open University Press in association with the
Centre for Socio-Legal Studies

Published Titles

Norman Lewis:	*Inner City Regeneration:*
	The Demise of Regional and Local Government
Michael Purdue	*Planning Appeals: A Critique*
Patrick Birkinshaw	*Reforming the Secret State*
Norman Lewis (ed)	*Happy and Glorious:*
	The Constitution in Transition

Forthcoming Titles:

Ian Harden	*Government Procurement Contracts*

Inner City Regeneration: The Demise of Regional and Local Government

by

Professor Norman Lewis

Edited by

Cosmo Graham

Open University Press
Buckingham/Philadelphia

Open University Press
Celtic Court
22 Ballmoor
Buckingham MK18 1XW

and
1900 Frost Road, Suite 101
Bristol, PA 19007, USA

First Published 1992

A catalogue record of this book is available from the British Library

Library of Congress Cataloguing-in-Publication Data
Lewis, Norman, 1940-
Inner city regeneration: the demise of regional and local government /
by Norman Lewis; edited by Cosmo Graham.
p. cm. -- (Studies in law and politics)
Includes bibliographical references and index.
ISBN 0-335-09632-8 (sc)
1. Municipal government -- Great Britain. 2. Urban policy -- Great
Britain. 3. Urban renewal -- Great Britain. 4. Central-local
government relations -- Great Britain. I. Graham, Cosmo. II. Title.
III. Series.
JS3118.L49 1991
320.8'5' 0941 -- dc20

Printed in Great Britain by J.W. Arrowsmith Limited, Bristol

Contents

Acknowledgement

I should like to record my thanks to the Nuffield Foundation, whose financial support made this project possible. Naturally the views expressed are mine and not theirs.

Norman Lewis

Abbreviations

AMA	Association of Metropolitan Authorities
BIC	Business in the Community
BR	British Rail
BRA	Boston Redevelopment Agency
BUD	British Urban Development Corporation
CAT	City Action Team
CBDC	Cardiff Bay Development Corporation
CBI	Confederation of British Industry
CLES	Centre for Local Economic Strategies
DE	Department of Employment
DES	Department of Education and Science
DOE	Department of Environment
DTI	Department of Trade and Industry
EC	European Community
ECSC	European Coal and Steel Community
FOI	Freedom of Information
FMI	Financial Management Initiative
HIP	Housing Investment Programmes
ICR	Inner City Regeneration
LDDC	London Docklands Development Corporation
LEA	Local Enterprise Agencies
NAO	National Audit Office
NCVO	National Council For Voluntary Organisations

NDC	Northern Development Company
NDPB	Non Departmental Public Bodies
PAC	Public Accounts Committee
PIC	Private Industry Councils
PSBR	Public Sector Borrowing Requirement
SDA	Scottish Development Agency
SE	Scottish Enterprise
SERC	Sheffield Economic Regeneration Committee
TEC	Training and EnterpriseCouncils
TNI	The Newcastle Initative
TPP	Transport Policies and Programme
TUC	Trades Union Congress
TVEI	Technical and Vocational Eduation Initiative
TWO	The Wearside Opportunity
UDC	Urban Development Corporation
UDP	Unitary Development Plan
UP	Urban Programme
WDA	Welsh Development Agency
WRFE	Work Related Further Education Programme

Inner City Regeneration: The Demise of Territorial Government

Summary

Recent years have seen a central assault on the powers of local government, combined with an increasing concentration of decision-making within Whitehall. However, given that government from the centre can never be effective without using agents or partners at the local level, the question is posed as to where both power and accountability lie for decisions taken up and down the country. This is a question of major constitutional significance in general terms but this essay concentrates on what some would call a 'legitimation deficit' in relation to the regeneration of our inner cities.

A process of de-industrialisation, among other things, has left many of our older cities in a state of serious decline, both economically and socially. It has become increasingly clear that market solutions on their own would not restore the integrity and prestige of the areas so afflicted. Government then has increasingly turned its attention to ways of regenerating, particularly, our inner city areas and has used a bewildering range of instruments for this purpose. Local government has found itself severely restricted in its ability to respond to the need for planned regeneration and instead central government has turned either to industry-led solutions or to the encouragement of partnerships of various kinds, with industry very much involved. For those who have followed such matters, one of the most striking phenomena in this area is the sheer complexity engendered by the range of initiatives and actors involved in the field. This produces a number of problems. The first is simply to identify who is doing what at any given moment. An anatomy of the major actors is called for, but is often very difficult to draw. An attendant problem is the likelihood that strategic planning will suffer with a myriad of different schemes in operation. Finally, we are faced with a serious question of constitutional accountability for what is happening in our cities. An increasingly opaque central government machine is exhorting industrial and financial capital, the community and volunteer movement, to a greater or lesser extent local government, and a clutch of quangos to act in the local interest. With local government not necessarily playing the central role it becomes exceedingly difficult to identify responsibility for action taken and not taken.

In the last few years a number of salient developments have been occurring in our inner cities and many dramatic improvements have been made. In spite of this, it is by no means clear that the best solutions have always been found or that there has been an intelligently integrated approach to social and economic development. There has been waste, there has been uneven progress and there has been a general failure to look at the needs of the region or sub-region systematically. Local government in many instances has done a great deal more than might have been expected under the circumstances. Nevertheless, it is entitled to feel frustrated at the lack of autonomy and resources required to correct years of neglect. Nor should we underestimate the contribution of private industry across a whole spectrum of activities which have benefited local communities. Even so, no broad body of electors elects the boards of major companies who, in any event, have their own imperatives to follow. There is no doubt in my mind that a clear legitimation deficit exists in this area which requires the regeneration of territorial politics, preferably within revised local government boundaries.

Chapter One
Introduction

The process of industrialisation, as many commentators have made clear, has been going through something of a sea-change in the last twenty years or so. The political science literature in this area is extremely fertile and little would be gained in an essay such as this by surveying that literature. One general statement, however, might be helpful as it impinges on the issue of inner city regeneration (ICR):

> The globalisation of the world economy meant a growing inter-relationship between its component parts. These reduced the spatial separation of countries and regions whose importance depended increasingly upon their position in the organisational hierarchy, particularly with respect to the location of control functions. Globalisation also made the constituent parts of the world economy more susceptible to the effects of international events such as the oil price rises and financial crises of the 1970s. The subsequent organisational, economic and technical structuring was evident in terms of rationalisation, spatial relocation and plant closure, mergers and acquisitions, and switches in capital/labour ratios. At the regional level, this meant the loss of entire and dominant industrial

> sectors, high unemployment and the growth of new, high technology and service activities elsewhere.
> (Bachtler 1990)

However this process is described, the urban problem is a problem since, in the United Kingdom as elsewhere, there has been a complete withdrawal of all private sector investment from some areas, while world-wide, manufacturing jobs constitute a declining proportion of employment in general. The United States and much of Europe has experienced similar, though by no means identical, problems. So, for example, Missouri enacted the Urban Redevelopment Corporations Law (Chp. 353 RS Mo.) in 1940 in recognition of this trend to localised de-industrialisation. This, in some senses, pre-dated much British encouragement of public/private partnership in conferring on private limited corporations some key public powers. These include the power of 'eminent domain', or compulsory purchase in British parlance. More generally, after World War ll, the various political groups in the Democratic coalition forged by the New Deal began to construct a national urban policy (Judd and Robertson 1988).

In any event, the 1980s in Britain were exhibiting signs of 'post-Fordist' stress exacerbated by deliberate economic and political policies adopted by government. That is to say that the old order of mass-production and standardised products was giving way to greater flexibility and specialisation. The old industrial heartlands were early casualties of this change which government action in Britain accelerated. Among those policies were included the enervating of local government through a series of legislative and financial measures to which I shall return shortly. However, the point that needs to be stressed here is that measures were urgently needed to redress a terminally deteriorating situation. We shall see that some confusion has surrounded the best way of achieving the regeneration of declining areas. Furthermore, the means adopted were not only likely to be challenged on the basis of their rationality, but also on the basis of their legitimacy. If local government was to play a less active role in these matters than the situation might seem to demand, then an alternative needed to be found which would command democratic respect. As a constitutional lawyer, this will constitute my primary focus. However, much other ground needs to be covered in the process. Nevertheless, procedures for drawing up, implementing and monitoring regeneration policies must be regarded as of the essence.

The Need for Regeneration

Unless whole areas of the country were to be abandoned to the vagaries of chance in an increasingly competitive world, it soon became clear that a process of positive restructuring was required. Partnerships between industrial and civic leaders and others were rapidly cobbled together in Britain as elsewhere. Indeed, the growth of corporate involvement in local economic development projects is both a European-wide and an American phenomenon (Blakely 1989). Nevertheless, there are different opinions as to the form and direction that restructuring should take. As Martin (1989) has pointed out, one area of debate concerns the relationship between regional and national economic policy. Some have argued that the most effective way of regenerating the depressed areas is to concentrate on policies to improve national economic growth irrespective of local needs. On this view, economic recovery of itself will provide the necessary impetus for local and regional regeneration. Whether this would do anything to improve the depressed areas relative to those which are more prosperous is another matter. One item immediately suggests a note of scepticism. It relates to the fact that most of the specialised business services tend to concentrate naturally in the larger cities with rich infrastructural and contact networks. For instance, most of the venture capital is in the South East, with sixty four per cent of funds located in London and a further thirteen per cent in the South East region (Brunskill 1989: 10). In fact, Britain has little privately based regional or local capital at all. More generally, it is clear that jobs have traditionally been somewhat more mobile than have people. In particular, corporations have become nomadic with many corporate headquarters moving away from their 'home' cities and therefore their employee base.

As to the form which regeneration should take, the jury is out, with no particular pattern readily discernible, save that at the moment private industry-led development is the Government preference. Social ownership is presently officially unfashionable, although it is too early to pronounce the demise of municipal enterprise, planning agreements, or social audits (Martin 1989). Furthermore, it would be a mistake to examine ICR from the point of view only of discrete initiatives or particular central government programmes. The Audit Commission in its 1989 report, for example, refers to the influence of central government in relation to geographical distribution; e.g. the national road building programme and location of airports (Audit Commission 1989: 64). Also of importance in this respect are government purchasing policies and decisions on the location of the civil service. The growth of Bristol and its connection with the defence industry is an example (Boddy 1988). These matters assume significance in relation to the scope of desirable territorial politics and the coherence of programmes and initiatives taken as a whole. From the point of view of a constitutional lawyer this has crucial implications for the institutions and machinery available for the assessment of such matters.

Another word of caution needs to be sounded. Government figures on public support can be misleading in relation to those items which are traditionally included and those not, and the general restrictions on local government finance which have occurred over recent years also need to be taken into account. Indeed, as long ago as 1986 it was being argued that the Urban Programme was largely self-financing since, in some cases, local authorities had lost around twelve times their urban programme allocations via the cuts which local government finance had suffered from the centre (AMA 1986). I shall not return to this issue again but it needs to be kept in mind when examining the overall picture. I shall have a little more to say about the Urban Programme in due course but it is worth making the point at the outset that its value has been declining rapidly while those parts of the urban investment programme which are under direct central government control have been rising. It is worth noting too that the Urban Programme in Wales has been steady in real terms for the past five years. I shall have occasion to remark from time to time that Wales is something of an aberrant case in relation to ICR, but it may be useful to put down a marker at this point. The significance of the Welsh experience will not be lost on those who see advantage in regional solutions and on integrated planning involving a wide range of interested parties.

Partnership: The Buzzword of the Eighties

The 1980s in Britain, and to a certain extent elsewhere, heralded an official hostility to old-style corporatism (Birkinshaw *et al* 1990). Partnerships, however, were *de rigueur*. A large range and assortment of partnerships have developed for the purposes of fulfilling numerous publicly-desired functions, but those between government and private industry have tended to be the most favoured. This is especially true in the field of ICR. However, before this point is developed, more should be said about the Urban Programme (UP).

The UP was the first major government programme to be targeted on the inner cities. It gives specific grant through local authorities to some 10,000 projects a year to help deal with special needs in urban areas. The key aspect is that it is targeted on priority groups and area local strategies drawn up by local authorities in consultation with the private sector and other groups. The 57 authorities invited to bid for UP funding are required to draw up inner area programme strategies. Individual projects have to support this strategy if they are to be approved for funding. Projects receive seventy five per cent grant with local authorities paying twenty five per cent. Inner area programme status has become extremely important both for obvious reasons and because it tends to act as a passport to other grants such as City Grant (Audit Commission 1989). This latter was introduced in 1988 at the launch of the *Action for Cities* initiative. City Grant encourages entrepreneurs to invest in urban areas where they would not do so otherwise. Grants are calculated as the difference between the costs and values of potential projects and are aimed at being the minimum necessary to persuade the developer to undertake a project. This has been accompanied by the Department of the Environment (DOE) assuming responsibilities that had previously been performed by local authorities. This involves helping developers to prepare formal applications, negotiating legal agreements with developers, processing payments, monitoring and assessment of completed schemes etc (National Audit Office (NAO) 1990). Even so, local authorities are consulted by the DOE as part of the formal project appraisal while developers are encouraged to contact local authorities to discuss planning, highways and so on. In Urban Development Corporation (UDC) areas, applications should be made direct to the UDC. Local authorities should also keep themselves informed about assistance available to private business so that they can direct firms to likely sources of finance and, where necessary, encourage applications themselves.

UP has scored many successes and is an indication that ICR is not really possible without considerable governmental assistance. Even so, the programme is not without its critics. The NAO has remarked that there is a great deal to be said for allowing local authorities' enthusiasm to influence the location of projects. But in some areas local authorities, efforts to attract investment have not been entirely successful due to a lack of interest by potential developers, and there are some indications that the demand for City Grant, in particular, will vary according to the state of local economies. Yet there are clear benefits from these grant regimes in terms of jobs, housing and the re-use of under used or derelict land. Government figures also suggest that the rate of gearing achieved by grants to industry is in the order of four to one. The picture seems, however, somewhat confusing since although City Grant is scheduled to rise in real terms, UP is continually falling. Furthermore, criticisms of the administration of the various regimes is not difficult to find.

The Audit Commission has remarked that the procedures through which central government administers UP and the criteria by which it assesses the submitted programmes, discourage local authorities from pursuing the aims embodied in ministerial guidelines. This is because government control over UP allocations is project-based, rather than focussing on the overall strategy being pursued locally. While supporting the concept of the UP, the Commission also pointed up other problems such as delays in programme approvals and over-detailed control of small projects. It also very helpfully suggested ways in which concerned local authorities could keep bureaucratic obstruction to a minimum (Audit Commission 1990).

One further preliminary point is worth making concerning official thinking on the relative importance of local government and industry. It is that expenditure on City Grant (a private industry-led programme) practically doubled between 1988-89 and 1989-90. This raises important questions about the leading role of industry and the relative importance of local government, quite apart from the ability of government at the centre to exercise rational influence or control. There is no doubt in the present climate that the role of industry is vital and will remain so. The question to be posed is how far industry can be expected to assume strategic responsibility for decisions and whether it can reasonably be expected to entertain social considerations and responsibility into the bargain. We have heard much talk of philanthropic responsibility in recent years but its limitations are all too apparent.

In March 1988 the Government launched the *Action for Cities* initiative as its main response to the problem of inner city decay (Cabinet Office 1988). It identified programmes involving expenditure of some £3,000 million in 1988-89 to support urban regeneration and suggested that more needed to be done to pull the various efforts together effectively. In 1990 it was followed by *People in Cities*, which spoke of an increase to £4,000 million and was confident that it was helping to create the conditions in which industry and commerce can thrive in the inner cities (DOE 1990). The document was greeted with a considerable fanfare and trumpeting and sought to bring together the vast and confusing range of programmes available for ICR. There was considerable Prime Ministerial support which sought to encourage private industry to engage in active partnership with others in order to pull the whole programme around. In January 1990 the NAO examined the main programmes available and considered three main issues: whether there were satisfactory arrangements for identifying urban regeneration needs and priorities, whether the delivery of relevant programmes was satisfactorily co-ordinated, particularly at the local level, and how far available information confirmed the effectiveness of the programmes examined. I shall return to these findings at a later stage but it is quite clear that essential questions were being asked and that the answers were not entirely satisfactory. Partnerships were and remain vital but strategic co-ordination is a prerequisite. That, however, is perhaps to pre-empt some of the things that need to be developed later. It is important first to say a little more about the nature and type of the partnerships in existence.

Social enterprise is not strong in Britain so that for redevelopment in the inner cities to occur public actors need to act in concert with private industry. Consequently the language of partnership is heard in almost every government utterance, though it is probably true to say that at the time of writing the co-ordinating role of industry is not called for as frequently as has sometimes been the case in the past. Instead we hear simply that business is crucial to inner city revival, that a partnership is needed between government, business, local authorities, voluntary organisations and, above all, local people. We are even assured that local authorities are increasingly sitting down with business to plan the regeneration of their cities (Cabinet Office 1989). Yet, not very long ago the CBI was speaking the language of business leadership in the cities:

> The Task Force recognises that calls for more co-ordinated leadership from the public sector are not the answer. Even if it were organisationally feasible to get the different players under one command the *commercial* investment would be limited at best. Mobilising private-sector funds on the scale required will be achieved only by harnessing the enterprise and management of the best business leaders in the community. Only they can create the confidence to draw in other private sector investors. (CBI 1988)

Those were, perhaps, especially heady moments and now the tone is gentler; the role of others is seen to be vital. The fact remains that we seem to move from grand government initiatives to grand business initiatives to genuine partnerships which are supposed to come about one knows not how. For business to take strategic responsibility for regeneration it would require a formidable body of information and would need to expend an enormous amount of time. This is not feasible so that *genuine* partnerships are spoken of more frequently, even if the strategic leadership is not adequately identified. Be that as it may, similar patterns are discernible, for example, in the United States. I shall have cause to return to these matters from time to time but the spectrum of types of partnership is just as much in evidence there. Let me give three examples. In Saint Louis, which is not as fashionable as many great American cities, business has a much easier time imposing its preferred version of development than the more sophisticated checks and balances to be found in Boston, where most multinational giants seek some kind of presence in a land-hungry primary development area. Meanwhile, in California, the liberal middle classes have been able to impose notable constraints on the ability of industry and commerce to develop willy-nilly.

The other point worth making briefly is that ICR is about more than business and commercial development. There are enormous social problems to be dealt with from housing and education, social welfare, combatting crime and the like. Business can clearly help with many of these matters but has neither the expertise nor the inclination to address them in the round. Indeed, even the Urban Development Corporations (UDCs) had been heavily criticised in the early years for failing to take into account the raft of social issues which needed to be grappled with in their areas. At the outset it was argued that others had statutory responsibility for, housing and education, so that a 'total' approach involving the human side of regeneration was unnecessary. That, fortunately, has begun to change so that in Docklands, for instance, the talk is now of investing in the local community through substantial social housing projects, training and education, environmental and landscaping schemes and so on. During 1989-90, for example, the London Docklands Development Corporation (LDDC) contributed £900,000 to primary education in its area and over £1,000,000 at the secondary level. It has also assisted with the refurbishment of housing estates. From being the target of considerable local abuse for its neglect of any but the commercial development of Docklands, it now openly speaks the language of community development. It speaks proudly of the need for balanced housing profiles and for local people to benefit from the opportunities provided by regeneration (LDDC 1989, 1990). The same note is struck in Wales by the Cardiff Bay Development Corporation (CBDC):

> The 'Community Development' approach should aim to make local people better able to identify needs and priorities and produce programmes of action. CBDC should establish a systematic means of consultation and of producing, appraising, monitoring and evaluating proposals. CBDC will need to work with the old and new communities, leaders in social life, local authorities, statutory

bodies, voluntary organisations and specific interest groups.

The procedures and responsibilities *must be formalised, straightforward, equitable and unambiguous.* Crucial areas of attention will be access to education, business opportunities, employment and skill training, and community involvement in improving amenities, housing and environment. (CBDC 1988: 12)

It is for others to assess how effectively these aspirations have been realised, but it is extremely unlikely that any body of business people, however philanthropic, could assess such needs, let alone cater for them. *En passant*, it should be said that even where UDCs fulfil these roles adequately, their strategic vision and suitability will still be attacked by many for other reasons. I shall address these matters later.

In Britain, one of the preferred roles for the business community has been a kind of consciousness-raising about the need to regenerate our cities with a sense of responsibility and pride. To a considerable extent Business in the Community (BIC) falls into that category though it has, during its short history, been fully involved in a whole raft of activities. Even so, it has, to a considerable extent, been prominent in encouraging private sponsorship for ICR and in elevating a sense of corporate citizenship. Very recently the Wearside Opportunity has been formed and comes very much into this category in describing itself as 'primarily a publicity initiative aimed at promoting Wearside' (Nicholson 1989). However, it may last a little longer than some other initiatives.

If one concept has dominated government thinking on ICR in Britain in recent years it has been that of the UDC. I shall have a good deal to say about this during the course of this essay but one of the prime purposes of the idea was to spend public money on land and infrastructure in order to persuade private industry to invest heavily in areas of industrial decline. Needless to say, a UDC/industry partnership of some sort or another is of the essence in such circumstances. London Docklands is the 'flagship' and for all the criticisms which it has attracted, its public/private gearing ratio is now in the order of one to twelve. Each month more national and international companies arrive in London (LDDC 1989). In Newcastle there is 'Newcastle Quayside', in Cardiff Bay 'Atlantic Wharf' and so on.

Elsewhere a great deal of hope has been pinned on business leadership teams. BIC has referred to the existence of a dozen business leadership teams in operation in England alone. More than 270 companies have joined the Per Cent Club in which they agree to devote at least half of one per cent of their profits to work in the community (DOE 1990: 21). These teams have been influenced by the apparent early success of The Newcastle Initiative (TNI) launched in 1988 as a result of the CBI Task Force study into the role which business could play in urban regeneration. The Directors of TNI include representatives from the local education community, the local authority and the local City Action Team (CAT; see p. 51). Its role is primarily to identify flagship projects and to promote a public relations programme. After considerable initial publicity it is presently unclear how much TNI is producing. The Wearside Opportunity (TWO) looks at the time of writing to be more influential in its own area, being a partnership of leading Wearside business people working in conjunction with senior representatives of local government and the major agencies. It has been able to secure some of the funds designated by the Government as part of a rescue package following the closure of the Sunderland shipyards.

In beginning to map out some of the different forms which partnership takes I am already starting to outline the confusion that such a huge range of initiatives presents the researcher, though probably others as well. To mention the Training and Enterprise Councils (TECS) is to stir further the alphabet soup which has been almost randomly concocted. TECS are bodies whose responsibility for training and enterprise should be crucial in the years to come. Again they will need further comment, but they receive government monies which are to be administered by a board which will have a two thirds to one third private sector/others ratio. Even so, we shall see that most of them continue to be run, at least in the short term, by central government in the regions. They may turn out to be more a case of devolved governmental administration than the original partnerships conceived by the Minister of the time. However, the point is readily made that 'partnerships' are as much made by 'spin-doctors' as made in a constitutional heaven.

What has been less fashionable in the past ten years or so is partnership involving the trade union movement. The unions have been even less fashionable than local government. The question which is of interest to many is whether they will stage a come-back in the way that local government appears to be in the process of doing. The TUC has constantly taken the view, not only that local authorities should be the main agents for economic regeneration, but that there is a requirement for strong regional planning. I shall want to argue later that there is some evidence that representatives of organised labour are being re-included in a number of bodies and working parties even where the representation on formal bodies has been diminished. This is especially true in Wales and Scotland where a culture of nationalism/regionalism may not only be beginning to swim with the new times but may be an indication of more strategically positive partnerships than some of those I have touched upon. In Wales, the Welsh Development Agency (WDA) has been extremely important in the fifteen or so years since it was established. Its board is largely employer dominated, though there is a trade union representative. In the last year for which I have a report new records were achieved in inward investment, business counselling services and land reclamation. The Chairman had this to say about the need for partnerships;

> We will continue to seek ever greater cooperation
> with the private sector, Welsh Office, other Agencies
> and local authorities to ensure the Welsh team is as
> effective as possible. (WDA 1989)

One more example is worth mentioning. In 1988 a Senior Training Group was formed for training and employment in South Glamorgan which indicated considerable vision and which took on board all significant interests in the region. The UDC may have been given the Government's brief, but at the local level they seemed to know that the old networks could not be by-passed. It is a lesson not lost on the United States, where it has been argued that successful economic development requires a network of key groups and individuals that encourages communication among leaders and facilitates mediation of differences among competing interests. This contributes, in this view, to continuity of policy (Blakely 1989: 262).

The Scottish Development Agency (SDA) has also achieved some striking successes, not least in conjunction with private industry, though its altered status at the time of writing leaves the future somewhat uncertain (Boyle 1988).

In summary, partnerships of various sorts are clearly important though a strategic hand has often not been obviously at work. Central government has taken important initiatives but has not been consistent, rational or coherent. Therefore, some partnerships have been worth more than others and the need for government to govern, while taking all views seriously into account, has been the biggest lacuna in recent years. In spite of this, a number of experiments have been undertaken which ought to be monitored. The Birmingham Heartlands project is one such, the strategic Sheffield 2000 is another. At the grass roots level a lot of attention has been paid to the Cruddas Park Estate in Newcastle, to which I shall also return. However, this experiment in community politics was made possible in part through TNI and its involvement has helped the local community to bring pressure to bear on its own local authority and upon the statutory authorities more generally. In any event it seems clear that private funding on the scale required to change the face of decay follows public money (Brunskill 1990: 19). The public face of government has a responsibility to take the lead while involving as many interested parties in as rational a fashion as possible:

> Almost all economic development depends upon public/private co-ordination and cooperation. It is essential that the pattern of these cooperative arrangements can be worked out carefully so that all parties know what to expect. (Blakely 1989: 263)

In concluding this introductory section, it should be said that local economic development throughout Europe generally has come about largely in a reactive fashion. There is almost no tradition of local economic capacity in this region of the world and it is almost certainly true to say that it has been the failure of central government to address the problems of economic decline and reformation that has brought about local economic activity (Blakely 1989: 287). Others have argued that not only has government placed too much faith in the ability of market forces to solve problems, but that it has failed to match the complex and interlocking nature of the problems found in urban areas with a co-ordinated inter-departmental and inter-agency response. There is, in this view, a need for a longer-term commitment, especially regarding infrastructure and the environment. This is allied to the fact that government has largely failed to provide an urban dimension to other policies such as industrial policy and defence expenditure.

To conclude, Britain is not alone in suffering serious economic alteration and reformation which has not been planned. The result is that communities established in the context of earlier periods of industrialisation have been severely damaged. The need for ICR has become widely apparent though coherence has scarcely been the watchword. Furthermore, there has been a tendency towards the marginalisation of local political communities in favour of market-led solutions. The rest of this essay is a detailed elaboration of these arguments.

Chapter Two
The Demise of Local Government

The relative 'demise' of local government over the last decade or so
has been, for the most part, the result of deliberate government policy.
Needless to say, if local government is taking fewer decisions than
formerly then something or somebody is stepping into the void.
Concerns with ICR have been strongly evident since at least 1977 and
require distinctly *constitutional* attention on account of their
significance and extent. This is, of course, because they fall outside the
mechanisms for rendering an account which were adopted for the
'dignified' parts of the constitution. Britain, being a nation of
constitutional 'trimmers' has reacted pragmatically both to 'extended'
government, corporatist styles of intervention and indeed much else
besides.

The relative demise of territorial politics (for we have little in the
way of regional structures either) and the growth of business-led
initiatives (quite apart from state-driven structures such as TECs) has
meant that a network of decision-making locations needs to be
identified. An anatomy of influence/decision-taking/policy
communities is required for obvious reasons, quite apart from the
equally important but less obvious reasons. If we have
aims/policies/objectives, we need to monitor them to see if there is
consonance between aims and outcomes; to see if they are effective
and to see if they are efficient. If we are high constitutionalists, if we

care about nurturing democratic ideals and if we care about active citizenship, then we shall need to monitor for perhaps different reasons. In any event, and whatever the concerns which drive our political system, we shall need coherent machinery and institutions for assessment; for channelling our inputs, for corporate planning and for monitoring outputs.

My main concern will be to examine the rationality of the machinery and institutions available for securing our objectives in the field of ICR. First, however, without dwelling on a subject which has been much discussed elsewhere, I need to say a little about the altered role of local government.

A Leaner Local State

Legislation in the field of local government in recent years is too numerous to mention, as is the series of economic interventions made by the centre on the periphery, so to speak. The Metropolitan Counties were, of course, abolished as was the GLC. Transport was de-regulated, local authority subsidies undermined, rate-capping occurred, local authority house-building almost ceased, land-use planning powers were diminished and so on. However, what is worth recalling is some of the ideology which has been particularly influential in the field of ICR specifically. Two public statements catch the flavour of the eighties. First, Mr. Nicholas Ridley as Secretary of State for the Environment in 1987. He explained to Tory backbenchers that items like the police and education apart, local authority spending had to be curtailed and that he wished to halt conventional investment programmes by local authorities in council homes, sports and leisure facilities and shopping centres. Councils should be allowed to stimulate such investments by the private sector but should no longer own them (*Guardian* 28 October 1987). Shortly afterwards the Prime Minister was reported to have instructed the Cabinet Co-ordinator for the Inner Cities, Mr. Kenneth Clarke, that the role of local authorities in running services should be substantially reduced. She expressed the view that if most services at the local level were privatised then not only would the role of the trade unions be broken but the role of local government itself would be reduced to a mere 'supervisory' service (*Guardian* 9 February 1988). This approach was remarked upon the following year by the Audit Commission, which reported that local government considered that central government thought it more appropriate that initiatives in the area of regeneration took place through the private sector, encouraged in numerous ways by central government:

> The absence of any but the most cursory mention of
> local government in the *Action for Cities* document,
> and government initiatives such as City Grant and the
> new Urban Development Corporations set up in 1987
> and 1988, which marginalise local authorities, have
> reinforced this view. Recent central government
> actions have suggested a more positive attitude.
> (Audit Commission 1989: 16)

City Grant is very much a case in point. It signifies the growing
centrality of private industry in the mind of central government though
it is increasingly becoming something in which the most active local
authorities are concerning themselves. The idea originally was that the
DOE should assume responsibility for a wide range of administrative
tasks previously undertaken by local authorities in which they would
help developers to prepare their applications for assistance (National
Audit Office 1990: 22). UDCs were invested with this responsibility
within their own areas. However, it has steadily become clear that both
the Department and developers are depending more and more heavily
on the co-ordinating role of local government in relation to these
matters, something I shall remark on frequently. It may be worth saying
that the Docklands UDC, which was heavily criticised in its early days
for lack of cooperation with local groups of all kinds, has now adopted
a Code of Consultation for its dealings with the respective local
authorities on its corporate plan (LDDC 1990: 10). It is worth adding
that, depending to some extent on how one does the sums, the
government's end of the urban programme expenditure is less than the
penalties imposed on local government through rate-capping and the
like.

Change is in the air in a number of ways, not least at the level of
the European Community. It has always been thought something of an
oddity that the Community has no elected regional representatives with
whom to deal in relation to for example, the structural funds. In reality,
the level of local authority involvement at the European level has often
seemed to be in the gift of national governments (House of Lords 1988:
14). Different ideological fashions will, in such circumstances, lead to
less than coherent decision-making.

In this area, things are not always what they appear. Thus, for
example, UP authorities are required to draw up an annual Inner Area
Programme to show what they are trying to achieve through the UP
and how this fits in with their overall strategy for economic,
environmental, social and housing problems (Audit Commission 1989:
43). In fact, most observers would remark that bids have been very

much project-led, with the skill being to sew a number of different projects together in what pretends to be, but rarely is, a pattern. In any event, the incremental nature of decision-making in this area, with Housing Investment Programmes bids being separate from Transport Policies and Programmes (highway bids) to take an example, has meant less pattern than would be desired. Even so, local authorities may have been down but few have been out. So, for instance, monitoring of urban development grant projects has relied very heavily on local authorities who were responsible for the administration of the scheme. More recently, there has even been official recognition by government that local authorities actually need a degree of freedom to tackle problems at the local level (National Audit Office 1990: 3, 16).

Wales: A Special Case

Although the changes in the shape and powers of government over recent years have applied similarly in most parts of the country, Wales seems to have been spared many of the excesses experienced elsewhere. It is true that the Cardiff Bay Development Corporation appears to represent a challenge to local government in the area, but a number of important differences can be detected from some of the other UDCs. It is the only one not to possess land-use planning powers; a clear concession to the work of, especially, South Glamorgan County Council in its long-standing attempts to develop the natural advantages of the Bay. Indeed, the urban development grant for Atlantic Wharf and the Distributor Road was the biggest ever by far in Britain and was agreed between the Welsh Office and the local authorities. Accordingly, local authority representation on the board of the Bay is strong while, elsewhere, surprisingly enduring links between business, the trades unions and politicians have been retained both in terms of training, development and other matters of interest. Welsh politics seems very much more consensual and networked than has been the general fashion elsewhere in Britain in recent years so that even if groups like the TUC are left off government-type bodies, they are still likely to be represented in working parties, sub-committees and the like. Furthermore, the existence of both the Welsh Office and the Welsh Development Agency have rendered the Principality much more resilient than some other parts of the UK. A number of these points will be developed elsewhere since, occasionally, there appear to be lessons to be learned for the business of ICR as a whole.

A surprising illustration may be worth mentioning in the form of the Cardiff Valleys Rail Strategy which is a programme agreed between BR, South Glamorgan and Cardiff City Councils (British Rail 1988). It relates to new ventures rather than the improvement of old ones, the intention being to improve services to the wider community; to improve access to employment from the valleys, to enhance tourist potential and to assist in meeting the social and economic objectives of the two counties as expounded in their structure plans. In highlighting the close relationship between transport and land-use policies this serves as a timely reminder of the importance of integrated economic planning. The project had to be agreed with the Welsh Office under a scheme which gave certain advantages to projects of regional and national importance which, *inter alia*, allowed local authorities to borrow beyond their cash limits. The significance of such developments has not been lost on the Audit Commission which simply notes that 'In Wales local authorities liaise with the Welsh Office on most matters'.

What I shall want to argue is that, whereas local authorities in England generally have been suffering considerable setbacks over the years, they now seem at least to be staging something of a comeback. In Wales, they were never really out of the picture. The close-knit nature of the political and social community and the existence of levels of para-regional government managed to prevent that. Perhaps this has significance for the general re-ordering of territorial politics in the UK over the longer term. In any event, one thing is clear. Local government is a key player. The question to be asked is how big a role it should be asked to play.

A Role for Local Government

Unfortunately for many of our public affairs, there are often too few continuous policy threads by which we can be guided. Fashions tend to change and slogans replace coherent patterned thought. ICR presents as good an example as any, where corporations and trusts are suddenly the answer to our problems, closely followed by business-led solutions only to be followed by 'partnerships' of various unspecified varieties. The permanent voice of the people during this period, local government, has often attempted to be heard, has often been ignored and has often been silenced. At the time of writing, however, at least in the short term, local government seems to be back in business.

The CBI report, *Initiatives beyond Charity*, recognised that local authorities are major players in terms of ICR and spoke of creating a partnership between the public and private sectors as well as involving the wider community. Even so, there are numerous references to the business community providing the leadership. Indeed, they go so far as to say that it is unrealistic to expect local politicians to be able to fulfil that leadership role alone:

> If local politicians cannot normally be expected to

provide the visionary leadership required, neither can central government ministers nor their departmental officials. Any worthwhile initiative will have to be *local*. Solutions imposed from the centre without the support and involvement of the local community are unlikely to succeed. The local business community must therefore step up to the responsibilities of leadership. (CBI 1988)

Well, some of this follows and some of it does not, and in fact the role of business in the community can be seen across a broad spectrum. The CBI document talks of a 'Good Corporate Neighbours' policy, but this is clearly capable of many different meanings. Business involvement may take the form of secondments for training and financial advice purposes, may involve publicity-driven consciousness raising for giving a region a higher industrial profile or, in some cases, involve it in a planning forum with representatives of the local community. However, the CBI Task Force not only seemed to be saying a number of contradictory things, but also to be making claims which are somewhat over-inflated.

At one point, it is possible for the CBI to say that if every business in the UK belonged to the 'Per Cent Club' (whereby a rising percentage of profits were ploughed directly back into the community) and all the funds were channelled into ICR, the resources would fall well short of what was needed:

For the solution lies far beyond charity. Private sector funds must be attracted into the cities on a truly commercial scale - and as a commercial investment, providing returns at least equal to those forecast for the alternative projects available to the corporate sector. (CBI 1988)

This is an extremely important statement which nevertheless indicates to me that this achievement cannot occur without public steerage. Yet:

The Task Force recognises that calls for more co-ordinated leadership from the public sector are not the answer. Even if it were organisationally feasible to get the different players under one command the *commercial* investment would be limited at best. Mobilising private-sector funds on the scale required will be achieved only by harnessing the enterprise and management of the best business leaders in the community. Only they can create the

confidence to draw in the private sector investors.
(CBI 1988)

The thrust of the CBI Report is that business leaderships need to indicate to public authorities what the real priorities should be. At the risk of tiring the reader, I shall need to pursue this theme for a little while longer since the issue is crucial:

> The main burden of the leaders' role will be to remove obstacles to the process. Conflicts between the public and private sectors will need resolving; priorities will have to be decided in the choice of development schemes. (CBI 1988)

The message is unmistakable. Although local government, for example, is a major player - in terms of housing, land, planning powers - and whose cooperation is therefore essential:

> Integrated development plans for related city sites should be prepared by retailers, house builders and industrialists, and should be given priority consideration by local and central government for grants and planning permission. (CBI 1988)

What is interesting here is that the CBI Task Force recommends that local authority chief executives join these various private sector groups, suggests local authority secondments and the like, but is cooler on the involvement of politicians. One assumes that bureaucrats share the same technical world-views. Be that as it may, there are severe problems here about democratic deficits. Quite apart from this, there is little evidence to suppose that most businessmen have any real interest or vision in the wider community over the longer-term, a matter for which the former Prime Minister, Mrs Thatcher, apparently berated them after the launch of what was, at the time, a very glitzy programme initiated by her and the CBI. Somewhat of a casualty within this programme was the British Urban Development Corporation (BUD) which committed itself at that time to seeking out new inner-city areas to develop. Three years on, in 1991, the collapse of the construction industry has meant the collapse of many of BUD's hopes. Its headquarters had moved from the West End to Greenwich, its staff cut from twelve to six and it had withdrawn from the £600 million scheme to turn Teesside into the chemical capital of the world. What also needs to be recalled is that the urban problem is a problem, in Britain as elsewhere, because there has been a complete withdrawal of all private sector investment from some areas. There is no doubting the importance of the business community to the regeneration of our cities but neither democracy nor the historic record suggests that it should take the lead role.

There is little doubt that the emphasis is beginning to change, even though the language employed is often only subtly different. Even so, it is worth remarking on the fact that two-thirds of metropolitan authorities have provided financial support to local business and that four-fifths have provided advice services (Audit Commission 1989: 37), that land assembly is often a key area where the local authority role is crucial (Audit Commission 1989: 67), that the South Glamorgan County Council *Action Report* in 1977 provided the primary impetus for the development of Cardiff Bay and that the Birmingham City Council Economic Strategy is currently having a very significant impact. A point to which it will be useful to return is that local authorities still have strategic responsibility for the development of land in their areas, a responsibility which many local authorities are now carrying out with an acute awareness of the needs of economic development.

There are those, of course, who have consistently taken the view that local authorities should be the main agents for regeneration in the cities, albeit in partnership with industry and the wider community (TUC 1988). It has been argued that their suitability to play the lead role lies in their position as major statutory bodies providing services; being employers, purchasers and landowners; being closer to the people who live in urban areas to identify problems and possible solutions; that they are uniquely placed to provide procedures for consultation and community involvement in decision-making and much else besides:

> local government is the only tier of government which
> is sufficiently responsive to the needs and problems
> of urban communities to play a leading role in the
> development and implementation of urban policy
> (Association of Metropolitan Authorities 1986: 8, 16)

What is interesting is that the more professional the analysts who examine ICR, the more insistent they seem to be on the role of local government. This is clearly true of the various government 'auditors', as we have seen, but it is found in the same measure in the work of private planning and financial consultants (Cardiff Bay Development Corporation 1988). Not only do the better authorities presently alert developers to likely sources of finance on their own initiative but they are formally now being advised to do so (Audit Commission 1989: 37). Interestingly, even in the buccaneering homeland of the entrepreneur, the United States, something of the same phenomenon is beginning to emerge. Without over-simplifying a complex situation, not only has local economic development taken root in general terms (Blakely 1989) but in some of the major cities, public authorities are at the heart of development strategies (for example, BRA 1982).

What is now detectable, furthermore, is the apparent change of heart of central government in these matters, if in few others. The DOE's most recent update on progress speaks of local authorities playing a 'key' role and disclosing 'co-operative' attitudes (DOE 1990: 22). Furthermore the Audit Commission's 1989 *Economic Development Audit Guide* dealing, *inter alia*, with local authorities' relations with other agencies has received Departmental approval. This seems to have coincided with a new approach to UP monies, concerning which ministerial guidelines seek 'to encourage local authorities to develop a co-ordinated approach and an action programme to tackle the problems of their inner areas' (Audit Commission 1989: 33, 37).

What is most significant, however, are parts III-V of the Local Government and Housing Act 1989. The Act requires local authorities proposing to undertake economic development activities to publish a statement each year describing those activities, the net costs incurred, and what it is hoped will be achieved. They must also consult appropriate bodies on the proposals before they are implemented (Section 35). The Act may well become important for a number of reasons. It introduced for the first time a specific power for local authorities to undertake a wide range of activities which they consider appropriate to promote economic development. Previously those who engaged in the promotion of economic activities relied upon a variety of specific and general powers. That, in itself would constitute a landmark, but just as important is the requirement for what is, in effect, a strategic document (following Departmental guidelines) required to be produced after consultation. In respect of the guidelines available, the proposals of the Audit Commission are clearly the most helpful and the most cognisant of the need for integrated strategic planning across the service departments and across the various layers of government.

The obligations come into effect for the first time for the period 1991-2. It is therefore too early to make a proper assessment of the full impact but already some authorities propose to make a series of further statements throughout the year setting out the authority's attitude to such matters as tourism, the environment and so on. As to consultation, I shall simply take the example of Newcastle on Tyne which engaged in a two-stage consultation process with eight primary organisations, though others were encouraged to respond and their views would naturally be addressed. The groups were fairly predictable for those who know the area and included the CBI, the

Chamber of Commerce, the UDC, TEC and various forums and initiatives, not forgetting the academic community. The work was undertaken by the Development Committee and the proposals were designed to mesh with other policy documents, in relation, for example to transportation, equal opportunities, the environment and the draft Unitary Development Plan. In Newcastle the document was broken down primarily into three aspects; image building, infrastructure and enterprise. It attempted to absorb and make coherent a wide range of activities involving a wide range of actors, from English Estates, through TNI to the European Community. As highway authority, it produces an annual Transport Policies and Programme (TPP) and has recently voluntarily assumed responsibility for producing an environmental audit. An attempt has been made to produce a strategic overview which embraces all the responsibilities and plans.

While I shall have much to say about the lack of overall coherence of ICR over the years, this development represents not only the most encouraging step taken so far, but also signals the re-emergence of local government from the shadows, at least in this respect.

Lessons for Local Government

Local government has been under considerable pressure for some years and remains so at the time of writing across a series of fronts. It is just possible that things may be improving for it in the field of economic development. We shall have to wait and see. However, it is clear that local government itself has not been blameless and has had to absorb a number of uncomfortable lessons in recent times. There are still some to be learned and it may be appropriate to conclude this chapter on that note.

There are a number of criticisms that can be levelled at local government historically. The first, perhaps, is that of paternalism and not responding to community needs through broad processes of consultation (Lewis and Harden 1982). The second is that, in many Labour-controlled areas particularly, there has been hostility to industry and commerce, much of it fuelled by the rating system. The third significant criticism is a common inability to act in a corporate fashion so that cross-departmental strategies were fulfilled. This, in turn, led to failures of monitoring and evaluation. How much of this has changed and what still remains to be done?

There is some clear evidence that the onslaughts of central government have caused local government to seek support from its own constituency so that electors know the hardships being faced by their representatives. This has, in many ways, been beneficial even if much consultation and community work has been tokenist. I have spoken to community workers and neighbourhood groups in many of our inner cities and remain convinced that much of the community development side of ICR is indeed tokenist and undertaken for public relations purposes. I shall come back to these matters later but flag something of what I have to say by reference to the celebrated experiment at Cruddas Park in Newcastle on Tyne. Cruddas Park was a classic sink estate; viciously high unemployment, high crime, social isolation, high child abuse and no community infrastructure. It would be reductionist to blame the local authority for this state of affairs but the sense of isolation felt by the residents included their relations with the town hall.

This was the situation found by Business Action in the Community (part of TNI) which decided that it needed a victim to champion, though the local authority does not totally share their version of history. As a result of the initiative the Department of Employment seconded an officer to conduct an estate 'audit' (with city council approval). This included a business and skills audit bearing upon businesses within a mile radius of the estate. This report was produced in February 1990 after public discussions had taken place with the local authority, the estate residents and TNI, to whom the report was formally submitted. A 'total issues' package was presented which was instrumental in setting up a steering committee of residents, establishing a Community and Enterprise Centre with a full-time community worker funded by the private sector and much else besides. The Centre is currently funded by the Department of Employment (DE), Barclays Bank, the Economic Development Committee (EDC) (with partnership funding from the DOE), the European Social Fund and other small amounts of private monies. The Centre displays job adverts, operates the Re-start Programme with positive counselling, especially through the community worker who is part of social and community services. At the time of my visit in late 1990, 106 residents had been found work and 200 had taken up training programmes. Community enterprise and workshops were planned as was a women's group.

Whatever the future of the estate, the achievements made in a short time have been remarkable. The community worker, who presumably will shortly be moving on, is a highly skilled and motivated professional of the sort who would succeed in any walk of life. His presence has probably been crucial, but the unlocking of the skills of the local residents has been remarkable to observe. The steering group first established at the outset has now become a Community Council with sub-groups concerned with housing, youth projects, a minority support group and so on. Most importantly from the present perspective, regular meetings with the local authority and statutory agencies have been established. These particular people have been put back in touch with their 'governments'. This could have happened before and did not; it may or may not be replicated or replicable. It probably was assisted by being supported by the business community to whom it could turn for leverage in a number of different directions, including roadblocks with officialdom. I shall return to the implications of this experiment later in the essay (Cruddas Park 1989, 1990).

There is an enormous body of literature and empirical evidence which indicates that not only can government not effectively run its programmes from the centre but that the periphery needs all the information it can get at the local level to make its decisions effective (Birkinshaw *et al* 1990, Lewis 1991). This has important implications then for local as well as central government, especially for its links both with business and the wider communitarian movement. As to the latter, there is some evidence that local communities can play an active and effective part in ICR, as witness the recent history of Boston, Massachusetts, to which I shall return (though see also Newcastle City Council 1991). However, it may be worth stating that Boston has studiously sought to reduce the number of bodies with which both developers and the local public have to deal in registering their observations over these matters. This returns us, of course, to the issue of corporate planning within authorities. This is a matter to which the Audit Commission has also drawn attention in urging that economic development is seen by the whole council as a central part of its strategy (Audit Commission 1989: 39).

Whatever the chequered history of the recent past there is now some clear improvement in the relations between local authority and business in many areas as the Audit Commission has pointed out in a number of its publications. Sheffield and Birmingham were singled out for favourable mention in attracting inward investment, although it is clear that many other authorities could do more to approach industry directly rather than waiting for them necessarily to make the first move (Audit Commission 1989: 80, 99). I shall return to some of these issues again, but Sheffield also serves as an example of co-ordinated decision-making where an Economic Regeneration Team exists which is a Chief Officer sub-group of the Management Team (Sheffield City Council 1990).

Economic development is perhaps beginning to come of age in the regions of Britain, with local authorities looking as if they will play an increasingly important part. It has not been easy for them for the reasons already touched upon, quite apart from the need to live with the European Community which, only recently, changed the rules relating to the structural funds. There is, however, some way to go before things can be said to be as rational and coherent as they might be. As to the general issue of accountability through the democratic processes, more needs to be said. One hope must be expressed, however, even at this juncture. It is that when the UDCs come to the end of their useful lives, their role and functions will revert to the realm of democratic territorial politics rather than be replaced by some amorphous 'Trust' or other hybrid (Cardiff Bay Development Corporation 1988: 94).

Whether the 'demise' of local government presaged the appearance on the scene of a whole range of actors to assist in the conduct of ICR or whether a relatively autonomous local government would have needed quite the same raft of partners is an open question. However, the bewildering range of actors on the ICR stage needs now to be addressed.

Chapter Three
The Range of Actors

The first thing that strikes an outside observer when attempting to chart an anatomy of the central players in the various ICR initiatives is the sheer range of both actors and initiatives. This is, of course, confusing. As you become more steeped in the 'regeneration game' the more this first impression is confirmed. There is, in fact, a huge market of agencies, easily capable of falling over each other. This sentiment is expressed by many who themselves are important figures within the ICR business, not least some of the members of CATs to whom I have spoken. A proliferation of decision-makers and levels of responsibility can rarely be justified, but in this case, in spite of manifest individual successes which can be identified, it is obvious that this range and complexity imperils coherent audit or monitoring initiatives. That is, if someone with interest and responsibility in doing those things can be found.

It is one thing to encourage experiments in living and markets to flourish; it is another to require strategic responsibility for the needs of an inner city. It is not immediately obvious, for example, how responsibility for community care, housing and the like can be separated out from ICR as a distinct animal. This is not the place to cover the ground reserved for the next chapter but the issue does at least need to be flagged. This major question is perhaps first officially posed in the Audit Commission's Report in 1989 on the local government dimension of urban regeneration and urban development:

> The most critical need is for the three major actors in urban regeneration - central government, local government and the private sector - to pull together. This does not always happen now. (Audit Commission 1989)

More recently the NAO voiced similar concerns saying that government departments have no overall assessment of inner cities special requirements and that programmes depend heavily on networks of contacts at local level. They said that performance varies and that there is scope for better communication. Furthermore, they found that there was insufficient information to assess the strategic impact of the various programmes and initiatives involved. In a study on innovation-related initiatives in Newcastle on Tyne, twenty one different policy measures were identified. It concluded that, although ideas were not difficult to come by, there was a distinct lack of co-ordination between the numerous single input policies and the other components of economic development such as finance, training, research development and premises.

The Role of Government

There are, plainly, several government departments involved with ICR; principally the DOE and Department of Trade and Industry (DTI), though the Department of Employment is also an important actor as is the Home Office with its responsibilities for the voluntary sector while the Department of Education and Science (DES) also has an interest in terms of the linkage between training and education. From time to time, there have been distinct governmental, even Cabinet, initiatives and at the moment a series of individual ministers has special responsibilities for certain of the partnership cities. However, even here there is a distinct lack of true coherence; hence the need for CATs and Task Forces, about which more later.

The DTI is mainly active through the Enterprise Initiative which is said to be a 'comprehensive package of DTI services to help enterprises of all kinds to build for the future' (DTI 1990). However, to cause greater confusion, most of the initiatives are broken down into sectors and are managed, or assisted, by such bodies as 3is (Investment in Industry), the Design Council, the Production Engineering Research Association, the Chartered Institute of Marketing, the Science and Engineering Research Council and so on.

The centrality of the DOE in relation to regeneration hardly needs comment. Suffice it to say that it has the primary responsibility for City Grant, UDCs, the Urban Programme, derelict land grant, land registers and enterprise zones (DOE 1989). There are so many other ways in which it, as well as the DTI, is involved in the regeneration process that it would be tiresome to catalogue them. However, a word or two might be said about the Estates Action Programme, not least since it operates according to a philosophy which involves many other agents than the local authority. Its main thrust is to attempt to transform unpopular council estates into places where people want to live. It provides extra resources to this end in order to strengthen and introduce local management which gives residents a greater role, to diversify tenure, attract private investment from building companies and others, and so on (DOE 1990). It is driven in part by the same motivation as the Housing Action Trusts which have been something of a lame duck so far. That aside, the DOE is, of course, the lead Department in terms of responsibility for local government in England.

These matters apart, a word or two needs to be said about *Action for Cities*, an initiative launched by the then Prime Minister, Mrs Thatcher, in 1988. This was intended to indicate a more corporate approach to the problems of ICR than had been adopted before. We shall see that this was more honoured in its promotion than in its realisation. However, the tone was clear and unequivocal:

> When I launched the Government's Action for Cities
> initiative in March last year I said that we were
> embarked on a great enterprise which would carry
> our towns and cities into the 21st Century in much
> better shape. That enterprise is now well under way.
> (Cabinet Office 1989: 2)

The Report goes on to praise the developments in terms of encouraging private investment, improving infrastructure and training, improving housing, tackling crime and promoting the arts and recreation. By this time, partnership had become the new buzzword; a partnership between government, business, local authorities, voluntary organisations and 'above all, local people'. A year later, the DOE rather than the Cabinet Office was carrying the ball. It announced that:

> If central government is to be an effective partner at
> the local level then it must have an effective
> mechanism for co-ordinating the delivery of its main
> programmes. (DOE 1990)

The answer, it seemed, was CATs. No matter that there were only eight; no matter that they were severely underfunded. Moreover, the appointment of a team of nine ministers to service these, and related projects, was supposed to show that a corporate approach was still being adopted, in spite of the lack of responsibility for ICR by a member of the Cabinet. Needless to say, none of the nine ministers could be regarded as household names. The lack of any real engine-room for driving the process of regeneration can be seen to be the more significant given, first, the sheer range of actors involved and, secondly, the contrasting signals emerging about who should be leading what kind of partnership at any given time.

Furthermore, as well as central and local government involvement, there is a strong presence from para-government, quango, Non-Departmental Public Bodies (NDPBs), call them as we may. A full list would be wearying, but of great significance is English Estates, which is an industrial corporation whose status is now statutorily defined (Industry Act 1980, English Estates Industrial Corporation Act 1981). It is England's largest developer and manager of industrial and commercial property, and operates principally in the assisted areas. Its aim is to stimulate economic activity and help to create jobs where they are needed most. The Housing Corporation too has become a major player and is the primary funder of housing associations. The money available to it from central government and elsewhere was expected to help in 100,000 house starts in the years 1990-93 (DOE 1990; the relationship between this programme and the Estate Action programme, not to mention Housing Action Trusts, will be passed over here in the interests of simplicity). Needless to say, the Corporation and associations work closely not just with government and the private sector, but also with the UDCs (LDDC 1990: 14). It is now time perhaps to say something more about the UDCs. The space available cannot do justice to their importance, and so a brief background statement and some broad propositions must suffice.

Urban Development Corporations

The UDCs have been at the heart of recent governments' regeneration strategies. They are administering a budget of well over £500 million in the current financial year compared with a total urban fund of some £900 million which is being steadily cut. Docklands alone accounts for over £300 million with Teesside, Mrs Thatcher's favourite provincial project, also relatively well-endowed (*Guardian* 4 February 1991). They are proving more expensive to administer than many had expected and there is currently some talk of their being asked to prepare 'exit' strategies. They were, of course, always intended to have a short life; to move in to a depressed area, clean it up and develop it, then to exit.

The UDCs, again American in origin, were clearly intended to signal the Government's lack of faith in local authorities; a provenance that has caused considerable problems as well as some measure of resentment. They were set the task of regeneration of their areas by bringing land and buildings back into effective use, encouraging the development of new and existing industry and commerce, creating an attractive environment and ensuring (though many thought this an afterthought) that there were housing and social facilities to encourage people to live and work in the area. Cardiff Bay apart, they possess land-use planning powers and are financed primarily by Exchequer grant, though they may borrow and plough back receipts, chiefly from land sales. Their Boards are appointed by the Secretary of State (DOE 1990).

Public monies have been pumped in to the UDCs in large measure since the private sector rarely undertakes land assembly, site negotiations with existing users or the provision of infrastructure (Cardiff Bay Development Corporation 1988: 76). The current government cash injection into Docklands, for instance, is intended to speed up the development of its road and rail links. The amount is more than double that which the Government had intended to put into LDDC over the next two years and appears to have alarmed the Secretary of State. In fact, the amount of public monies made available in and around UDC areas has often been disguised, not least in terms of improvements to the infrastructure, tax reliefs and the like (DTI 1989: paras. 16, 28). Indeed it has been argued, however accurately, that Canary Wharf has been developed with £900 millions of help being given to the developer responsible (*Private Eye* 23 November 1990). One thing is clear; the direct Exchequer grant does not tell the whole story.

On the other hand, the UDCs, especially in Docklands, have attracted very considerable sums of private monies into their areas. In 1989 the Public Accounts Committee was able to say that the LDDC had already attracted over two billion pounds of private investment, a figure regarded as a severe underestimate by the LDDC itself (LDDC 1989). In the same year, Tyne and Wear UDC could claim £250 million already committed by the private sector. What the picture would have been if the strategic responsibility were to have been lodged with a local tier of elected government we shall never know, but there is little doubt that the early years' experience of the UDCs disclosed serious flaws, while others would argue that the whole strategy was misconceived and essentially damaging.

The major criticism has been that the UDCs are concerned with their own patch without necessary consideration of the needs of the wider urban area of which they are a part. Liverpool is an example, though in many ways its experience has been unique. Complaints occur that, however successful the regeneration of the docklands area and the commercial quarter, it has not touched the lives of ordinary citizens in the inner cities (Merseyside Development Corporation 1989). Prestige projects have moved ahead with over £200 million being spent on the UDC area, while Liverpool's share of the UP has declined dramatically. Even two years ago the PAC could criticise the UDCs for defects in their corporate planning, monitoring procedures, failure to consult the local communities, under-playing social needs, bypassing elected representatives and some dubious accounting methods. A number of them have fallen victim to the property slump of the late 1980s and early 1990s. This may or may not be attributed to their game plan. Even so, one commentator reflects the concerns of many:

> The scale, size and scope of development has been determined solely by the developers' assessments of the needs of the market, rather than intentional planning criteria, such as environmental impact.

> In the Isle of Dogs Enterprise Zone, developers have been free to build anything they please, as high as they want and in whatever material they choose. Now, with land prices falling and developers seeking to minimise losses by pulling out, the market threatens to kill off its prodigy. (*Independent* 4 January 1990)

Others have commented on the bias in UDCs towards development of land and buildings rather than industrial policies for the regeneration of the existing economic base or the labour market (Centre for Local Economic Strategies (CLES) 1990: 22).

There have also been problems at Sheffield UDC where an internal investigation was put in train by the DOE after allegations about conflicts of interest (*Planning* 20 July 1990), and there has also been considerable criticism about the economics of its land purchasing policies.

However, many of the early lessons have been learned, so that most weaknesses which observers would now identify probably relate either to the concept of the UDC itself or to their overall briefs, which in some measure were conceived by central government. Tyne and Wear, like Cardiff Bay, has, at least, adopted a strategic approach to the area under its control, with project design briefs insisting that developments lead to improvements in the life of the local communities. Consultation of differing degrees of rigour has occurred in Tyne and Wear, in Sheffield and in Cardiff Bay, even if there is not the same community influence over developers that exists in Boston, Massachusetts. Nevertheless general improvements in the provision of social housing, relations with local government and the wider community, training provision *et al* have all improved dramatically in recent years. Cardiff Bay's regeneration strategy (bearing in mind the cohesion of the industrial/political community in that part of the world) has, some would say, also been a model of its kind. A series of middle-range development suggestions emerged within the framework of a larger development strategy with each of the main development areas becoming the subject of detailed planning briefs to guide development (see the various annual reports of recent years and Cardiff Bay Development Corporation 1988: 96).

It might seem churlish to criticise the UDCs for their general lack of openness compared to their counterparts in the United States, given the general culture of secrecy which characterises British government. Even so, the failure to publish corporate plans and the constant use of outside consultants whose findings are not made public does require mention (Public Accounts Committee 1989: 24, 32). What is also important to note is that the achievements of the two initial UDCs were not analysed before the decision to establish the second and third generation. This might suggest a closed government mind to some; it says little about the willingness to learn from mistakes.

What can be made of this enormously complex area in short? There are those who argue that a single-task agency can produce rapid achievements where traditional organisational forms are constrained by their cultures and by the rules of the game. Be that as it may, the advantage may be bought at too great a cost. First, a constitutional lawyer is bound to remark on the lack of constitutional accountability of UDCs appointed by Secretaries of State who favour business over local political leadership. The lack of an Administrative Procedure Act and other sub-Parliamentary constraints (Lewis 1989) simply exacerbates the problem which exists in Britain with all para-state agencies. A brief which is not directed at the whole urban, let alone sub-regional, set of problems is also bound to be subject to severe limitations from the outset. Add to this the fact that the strategies directed to the UDCs from the DOE might themselves be mistaken and it is going to be difficult to regard them as a major institutional contribution to the delivery of vital public policies. It is widely believed that the strategy imposed on the Merseyside Development Corporation prepared by DOE consultants was simply misinformed (PAC 1989: para. 5078). A strategy based on improbable industry and commerce was eventually replaced by one committed much more to leisure and tourism. Even in Tyne and Wear, which is, relatively speaking, a model of participation, consultation and community concern in so many ways, a siren voice or two can be heard to the effect that promoting development was the wrong strategy. It might have been preferable to improve the infrastructure in the expectation that development would follow the facilities. As it is, severe pressure is being placed upon, for example, the regional transport system. Lack of adequate partnerships between relevant tiers of government will almost certainly continue to muddy the waters in the short or even medium term. It is an open secret that in Sheffield the forum for partnership developed in the area (Sheffield Economic Regeneration Committee or SERC) sought government monies for a 'regeneration partnership'. They were refused and had to settle for the UDC instead.

Perhaps one of the most serious criticisms relating to the multiplicity of agencies and the consequent effect on strategic thinking relates to the effect of a market-led approach on local authority development plans. Where UDCs produce plans and strategy brochures aimed at attracting private development there is a likelihood that this will generate conflict with local authority development plans which are required to take into account both a wider range of factors and a wider geographical area. This can have serious effects on a host of issues, not least housing development (CLES 1990: 24-5).

This is not the place to conduct a disquisition on 'para' or extended government, but suffice it to say that, constitutionally speaking, its role is inadequately defined and regulated (Birkinshaw *et al* 1990). This is as serious a matter in the present context as in any other.

At this point, I need to say a little more about the role of business, although I shall return to the theme from time to time. Let me begin with the so-called 'Phoenix' initiative in 1986. This was a non-profit organisation substantially funded by the DOE and led by a steering group of businessmen ('task forces' were the preferred jargon two years later) from the private sector. Its aim was to bring together at city level different sectors into a partnership, while providing a national source of expertise, advice and information on regeneration matters. It became involved in an area in response to a request from local authorities or private sector organisations. It launched its inaugural programme in 1987 with a £70 million scheme to regenerate thirty five acres of central Manchester, to date easily its major achievement, providing its services as an independent intermediary which could co-ordinate the work of twelve developers. At the time of writing its primary medium for ICR is, perhaps rather confusingly styled 'Community Development Corporations', a 'pro-active partnership' between the public and the private sector often described as being in the business of development brokerage.

BUD has already been mentioned, but the CBI Task Force has also been a central player. This was set up in 1987 and the following year produced the Report already referred to and became Business in the Community, with overlapping membership from the main BIC Board and from Phoenix itself. The objectives included avoiding duplication of effort, pooling knowledge and sharing experience in the 'complex' business of regeneration. A core team was formed with the objective of supporting or helping to support Business Leadership Teams in various parts of Britain. In 1990 the DOE identified twelve such teams, most of them going for 'flagship' projects. Specific recommendations of the Task Force at one time were simpler and faster planning procedures, 'negative' public auctions for derelict or vacant land (i.e. the winner should be the one who wishes to receive the lowest subsidy), an increased role for private capital in public housing and closer links between business and council housing estates. In the longer term the expectation was that BIC should be the umbrella group under which all these activities could be co-ordinated. This is perhaps the place to say a little more about what has been one of the most significant developments in the field.

BIC, Flagships and Local Enterprise Agencies

In reality BIC, founded in 1981, is as confused as most observers on how to tackle the problems of ICR although it has made suggestions from time to time on how business can help; action through location and investment, through employment and training, through purchasing policy, through public affairs, community and charitable support and local partnerships (BIC/BP 1987). This is, of course, broad and unspecific, though more direct ideas have emerged, as through the Neighbourhood Economic Development Programme, launched in 1987, which seeks to increase opportunities for people living in neighbourhoods experiencing serious economic and social problems. Again, the documentation is high on generalities and low on specifics yet the degree of exhortation has clearly had some beneficial impact. The BIC *Review of the Year 1988* gives some flavour of their activity. In that year, eight Target Teams were set up, including members drawn from the 'highest echelons of business throughout the country'; the projects targeted included education partnerships, finance for enterprise, voluntary sector initiatives and so on. Guides, guidance and publicity all emerged from these initiatives. Also figuring prominently were the Business Action Teams, Local Enterprise Agencies (LEAs), the Youth Enterprise Centre Development Unit and so on. There are in fact nine regional offices of BIC around the country, as well their London headquarters, and a document of some interest is *Companies in the Community*, a set of guidelines for company boards on how they can contribute to community regeneration through mainstream business activity (BIC 1989). By 1989 BIC's emphasis had turned to the business role in training, which we shall return to shortly. However, the role of business in TNI, the Wearside Opportunity, and so on, was still being heavily stressed (*Business in the Community Magazine*, Spring 1989). Yet for all BIC's involvement in partnerships, flagships and the like, perhaps its strongest role has been in supporting LEAs.

The first LEAs were founded in the late 1970s and currently number around 300. They were originally formed as essentially local partnerships between the public and private sectors to offer free help and advice to small businesses. Their core activity is still free, confidential business counselling and support, mainly for 'micro-businesses', but increasingly for business with growth and potential, whether at the start of the expansion stage or not. BIC has been significantly active in promoting and sustaining the LEAs, though local authorities are still the most common financial sponsor, albeit closely followed by the corporate sector (BIC 1988a, BIC and British Telecom 1988). We shall see that the emergence of the TECs confounds still further the coherence of the enterprise side of local economic activity and, indeed, there have been adverse critical comments about the ability of private industry to take the lead even here and the confusion caused by the range of bodies in the advice and assistance game (Brunskill 1990: 18, 20).

In truth, although many successes have been recorded (Birmingham, Sheffield and Newcastle have all been praised for their business/local government partnerships), there has been no real national pattern and there is the strong feeling that business in general is unwilling and unable to take the kind of lead envisaged at one time. Even so, there is little doubt that corporate involvement in regeneration is alive and exceedingly active, even if the co-ordination one would have liked is not always present. Just to take a few examples; British Rail has a Community Unit and says that corporate community involvement is part of being a good employer in the 1990s. They support over 130 Local Enterprise Agencies in England and Wales alone. There were, in 1989, 54 BR secondees in the LEAs; the Bank of England has a strong secondment policy which is not specifically limited to LEAs, while Barclays Bank, British Petroleum and many others are all active in lending their support to community ventures (see *Enterprise World* December 1989).

At the time of writing, partnership is in favour (and I would go so far as to say inevitable), with no particularly clear framework being favoured, although the Audit Commission and the DOE have begun to produce very helpful guidance. The Heartlands Company in Birmingham is a model which has attracted much attention, including government attention, and presently the DOE is proposing to take a harder look at its experience to see what lessons may be available for other regeneration projects. It is certainly a most impressive initiative and one which so titillated the DOE that it resiled from its original intention to designate the area as a UDC. The Heartlands Company itself was intended originally to be a development company but has ended up acting as a facilitator of development in the area. The fact that its Board includes a number of developers active within Heartlands itself has, interestingly, not produced any signs of conflicts of interest. The local authority is not only a shareholder and represented on the Board but is a partner in every way. The Chief Executive, a man of singular energy and vision, had nothing but praise for the cooperation between the public and private sector which had become standard practice (Birmingham Heartlands 1989). It may be that further developments of this nature will be encouraged, but my own feeling is that, whatever the future and shape of public/private partnerships, the idea of business determining the pattern of regeneration is dying on its feet. However, before I return to the crucial issues of strategic responsibility for ICR, I must turn briefly to other crucial actors and issues; in particular the problems of financing development in the inner cities and education and training initiatives which have developed and are developing.

Education and Training

ICR includes more than industrial and commercial development. It includes, as we have seen, attention paid to housing and social welfare. It also necessitates attention paid to education and training for any new jobs which might emerge. To plan rationally these matters are crucial.

Amongst the most significant developments have been 'educational compacts' between schools and local employers. They were pioneered in England by the ILEA and the London Local Enterprise Agency, drawing upon American experience. This commits schools and pupils to a set of quantified goals, and employers to giving preference for jobs to pupils who meet those goals. Once more, BIC's involvement needs to be noted in helping to forge, through its Education and Business Partnership Target Team, a series of Education and Business Partnerships, being joint ventures between employers and the education services in a local community. It is a formal agreement committing the partners to work together to improve the employment and education opportunities of young people while meeting employers' needs for a well-qualified workforce (BIC 1988b). Other related initiatives, begun by the then Training Agency, now effectively absorbed back into the DE, include Technical

Vocational Education Initiatives (TVEI) and Work Related Further Education Programmes (WRFE). The former aims to prepare young people for working life by making what they learn at school more relevant to the world of work. Every education authority in Britain is now taking part in it and all young people between fourteen and eighteen are now supposed to have access to it. The main aim of the latter programme is to link vocational education more closely to the needs of employers. The programme provides incentives and help to the public sector of further education to help it to respond more rapidly to the changing needs of employers and to enhance the cost effectiveness of its provision.

However, what now complicates the matter is that TECs are in the process of assuming responsibility for Compacts as well as numerous other responsibilities of a training nature, some of them seeming to be 'social'. It is time, perhaps to say a little more about the nature of TECs (Department of Employment 1988).

Training and Enterprise Councils are again an idea borrowed from the United States, where they were called PICs (Private Industry Councils). Their British origins are the subject of much political gossip, but whatever the original intentions were, they seem to have been transformed. Even so, their function is to plan and deliver training and to promote and support the development of small businesses and self-employment in their areas. The core of their activity is to be the training and business assistance programmes previously run by the DE and the Training Agency. At the outset it was assumed that they would also play a major role in the wider development of the areas for which they were responsible. They are companies subject to ordinary company law, rather than having public law status, as do their continental counterparts, and operate under a performance contract with government. The directors of the company are to be appointed as individuals with equal voting rights and will receive no direct remuneration. The employees, at the moment of writing, are normally seconded from the Training Agency though there is some move to change this arrangement. It is too early, and the limited experience is too varied, to describe their natures, roles and functions precisely, which, in any event, would take a separate monograph to do it justice. Suffice it to say that the Sheffield TEC is not untypical in having ten private Board members, five public appointees (for example, city councillors), two trade unionists and the Principal of the City Polytechnic.

The major issues, accountability apart, are the nature of their links with the wider community, their response to training the less fortunate, whether performance indicators will dominate their activities as opposed to being able to tailor their programmes to fit local needs (reductions in finance presently are a worrying sign) and whether they will be able to move forward quickly from the initial DE programmes to a wider range of activities (Bennett *et al* 1989, DE 1989). Already there are mixed opinions about the ability and willingness of TECs to perform their educational responsibilities, some of which have been outlined earlier. They will, however, have to make sense of the myriad government and business initiatives on education, many of which duplicate each other and pursue the same goals. Some businessmen are already disenchanted by being constantly approached by schools to involve them in a seemingly endless series of initiatives. Oddly, although the relationships between industry and education seems to have improved remarkably over recent years, the Government, in designing TECs, seemed deliberately to be side-stepping local education authorities who, of course, have no legal right to be represented on the Boards (*Financial Times* 18 March 1991).

It remains to be seen how successful TECs will be; how responsive to local needs, how rationally they will fit in to the needs of the inner city programmes in particular and how far the influence of the DE centrally remains dominant. There is already one school of opinion which says that the Boards are icing on the Training Agency cake. The real decisions are Treasury-led and implemented by local (civil servant) management according to the demands of the FMI and Next Steps thinking (Jenkins *et al* 1988). This need not happen, as seems to be shown by the experience of Birmingham, but the pressures will probably be great.

Several things need to be said about TECs at the formal and institutional level. There are DE guidelines on the TECs' 'constitutions'. They operate under a contract with the DE and through contracts with the service providers. They also operate under a three-year rolling corporate plan, though their Treasury funding operates on an annual level. The original intention, exploded by the experience of PICs, was that private sector funding would begin to match the public funding in a short time, but that requirement seems to have been quietly dropped. TEC Board meetings are closed and their minutes are not published, though the contracts normally require one annual public meeting. Monitoring appears to operate at the level of a mass of monthly information sent to the region, but this, of course, is also subject to an annual business plan. It also looks as if increasing flexibility is being allowed to TECs at the price of reduced funding.

A General Operating Agreement between the Secretary of State for Employment and the TECs is in the public domain, though individual contracts appear to be commercial in confidence. Few variations, however, can be expected from the core operating agreement. This deals with the fact that at least two-thirds of the Board must be from the private sector (including the chair), that summaries of the corporate and business plans shall be published, while a copy of the full corporate plan must be made available at the TEC's registered office. Monitoring, audit and information and detailed financial obligations are also laid down in the contract. Some TECs make available a 'core' contract which they intend to use with their training providers, but the contracts themselves are commercial in confidence and would not be made available by the TEC itself, though in most instances there would be nothing to prevent training providers making this information public if they wished.

What conclusions can be drawn at this very early stage? Well, first that a 'contractual' arrangement with an incorporated body is an odd, but well-tried, way to conduct what is essentially public business. The relations with the wider community must be observed with interest, but accountability *per se* at the constitutional level is avoided by use of this mechanism. Although in some areas (and Sheffield is an example) there is a close linkage between the TEC and the broader partnership arrangements, the Secretary of State has prohibited equal membership between industry and local government. In those areas where strategic thinking is led by local government in partnership with industry and others TECs could yet be extremely valuable devices. However, at the level of constitutional politics, the emergence of TECs can scarcely be seen as an articulate and coherent response to the problems of the inner cities. Furthermore, TECs are one more major actor in the drama, in circumstances where we will have to wait and see whether simplification and rationalisation of the training and education process occurs.

Finance and the Inner Cities

Money is always, as Deep Throat notoriously once said, the key. In terms of public programmes there is never enough. We all, at the end of the day, die on the altar of Treasury financial rigour. However, there is a strong belief that considerable budget unfairness exists as between the regions. Few I spoke to in my discussions argued for full governmental responsibility for regeneration programmes and all were in favour of partnerships of various sorts. However, pump-priming is vital as, probably, is adequate loan finance on fair terms. If there is differential access to funds of all sorts in different regions there is bound to be dissatisfaction. This raises the issues of a rational and coherent regional approach to these problems; it is an issue that has been touched upon already and will form a strong focus of the rest of this essay.

Even so, the belief is that Wales and Scotland, for instance, especially through the Development Agencies, have received unfair advantages over the other depressed regions. These observations are as likely to come from the civil service as from local notables in my experience. We have already noted too that most of the venture capital is in the South East, where rich infrastructural and contact networks exist. Whatever the general weaknesses of the financial sector's commitment to the industrial sector, there is a specific reluctance to invest in the West Midlands and the North of England. What is needed, according to some, is the development of locally-based and locally-focussed capital markets to increase the flow and autonomy of regional investment funds:

> The progressive loss of regional independence and control over finance capital to London-based institutions over the past century needs to be reversed. Some movement is taking place on this front, with recent creations of a small number of private sector and local authority enterprise board investment funds in northern regions, but according to many observers the scale of the regional 'equity gap' is such that it should be considered as a key institutional element of the regional problem, and hence a primary target for regional policy. (Martin 1989: 41).

The establishment of regional capital markets is what is being argued for here, the logical concomitant of which is the regional development agency responsible perhaps to a regional form of government. But more of that anon. There are, apart from Martin's examples, some other investment players who need to be mentioned. The most important is undoubtedly '3is'.

3i is a unique private sector company, originated in 1945 by the Bank of England and the clearing banks to help meet British industry's long-term capital requirements. As such it claims to be the largest venture capital organisation in the world. It is characterised by its investment in minority shareholdings, leaving management in control of their business. The disproportionate investment in the South East is presently a fact of life but 3i has a network of 29 offices which have built up local expertise and contacts. Furthermore, as well as having international offices, it develops commercial and industrial properties in the UK by either developing sites or by acquiring existing properties for improvement and ultimate onward sale. It is also fair to say that recent years have seen 3i very active indeed, so that in the last five years it has invested as much as in the previous nearly forty years of its history. About five per cent of the companies in its portfolio fail every year, which is at least an indication that it is in the business of risk-taking. To take one further example, the Sheffield Office, opened in 1970, has invested thirty five million pounds in the last five years (see *Investors in Industry*, promotional package). There are, as might be expected, other financial backers of various kinds, of which I shall mention but one. It is the scheme jointly organised by Barclays Bank and the European Coal and Steel Community early in 1990 whereby a £90 million loan agreement was made with Barclays acting as the ECSC's agent. It was intended to provide subsidised finance for companies which could show that they were providing new jobs in areas hit by redundancies in the coal and steel industries (*The Guardian* 29 January 1990).

What I have sought to do in this brief section is to point out that there are also actors involved in the ICR drama whose business is finance for development, while at the same time introducing the idea that 'solutions' as presently envisaged are too piecemeal and unbalanced for the nature of the problems to be solved. Before returning to this second theme I want to say a few words about some other players or actors in our drama, some major and some minor.

Players, Players and More Players

Let me begin with some of the smaller schemes and institutions without wishing in any way to play down the significance of their activities. Again, there is no attempt to be exhaustive but only to indicate the profusion and confusion of activities. In no particular order they include: the Action Resource Centre which seeks to channel professional, managerial and technical skills to community organisations; Training for Community Enterprises; the Bridge Group, which is an alliance between national charities engaged in community economic development; the Groundwork Foundation which embraces a series of trusts established to promote the conservation, protection and improvement of the physical and natural environment in specific target areas; Common Purpose, whose aim is to educate key players from all sectors of the community in issues affecting their city. It seeks applicants from the public, private, voluntary and community sectors and provides a programme to increase their understanding of and impact on city life. Others are: Project Fullemploy, which seeks to establish training opportunities for the ethnic communities; Instant Muscle, to help disadvantaged people to form their own businesses; Livewire, Young Enterprise, the Prince's Youth Business Trust and so on and so on.

A word should also be said about the Industrial Society, whose concerns, as is well-known, extend far beyond the field of ICR. Even so, they have begun to play an active role in the inner cities, particularly as an organising and exhortatory force. Their *Influencing Change* programme for the Department of Employment is among their lead activities in this area, though they do have a separate Inner Cities Unit. It is a development programme for middle managers in the DE in collaboration with colleagues from other Departments, community and voluntary groups and others. It is closely linked to a series of workshops carried out in a single day to break down misunderstandings between the interested parties and to foster collaboration, where they believe there is currently a problem. Of further importance are their 'Headstart' projects, carried out through their Inner City Teams. The projects seek to open up to schoolchildren and young entrepreneurs the varied opportunities in work and self-employment. The DTI, Training Agency and five hundred, mainly private, companies have been involved. The projects are varied and include awareness of Government-sponsored training opportunities through placements in companies and start-up opportunities (DE 1989).

The Voluntary Sector

The voluntary sector, extremely difficult to treat homogeneously in any event, has become more and more significant in recent years in almost all aspects of public policy. The general thrust of this development has been charted elsewhere (Birkinshaw *et al* 1990, Lewis 1990) and so I shall concentrate, perhaps too briefly, on the vital role of the sector in the field of inner city regeneration, where it could hardly be more important. For present purposes I shall roll together the voluntary and community sectors.

There are, of course, many different kinds of voluntary organisation in urban areas. Some are charities, some are not. Some are branches of national organisations, some are set up locally. They have in common that they are established 'voluntarily', that is, neither by statute nor for profit. Nearly all are managed by local people serving on management committees, sometimes alongside representatives from a national voluntary organisation. Most urban areas have voluntary development agencies of one sort or another which provide information, practical resources, advice and training for local organisations and often put them in touch with others so that experience can be pooled.

National voluntary organisations have responded to the plight of the inner cities by bringing in ideas, resources and specialist expertise. This includes showing groups how to access resources, generating new resources, setting up counselling services, helping to prevent crime, running family centres to take pressure off single-parent families or those suffering from unemployment, setting up community enterprises, providing housing, especially for those with special needs, and providing help and support for homeless families and single people (National Council for Voluntary Organisations (NCVO) 1988).

Clearly, voluntary and community groups are increasingly important in the inner cities, though they are sometimes critical of the way their role is perceived. For example, NCVO has complained that too often they are consulted after decisions have been made, investment committed and vested interests lined up. It is not enough, they argued, to approach a local group three weeks before a facility opens since by the time local people are approached many opportunities have been wasted, while timely consultation can uncover potential difficulties which an outsider might not anticipate:

> Business and government often find the diversity of local activities and interests difficult to accommodate when planning new initiatives, but policies need to be able to respond to the differences within inner cities. A range of initiatives will bubble up from below, and the picture of local enterprise will appear rather messy to officials used to working within the known quantities of the bureaucratic system. The temptation to tidy it all up into a manageable system should be resisted, however, if the search is on for innovation choice and creativity.

> There is help at hand. Local development agencies can often guide outside agencies to local voluntary organisations and help them build an overall picture. They can also help to get information to different groups in a form that they can respond to. (NCVO 1988: 30).

The NCVO has estimated the annual turnover of voluntary organisations in the fifty seven Inner Area Partnership areas at £400,000 in grants and trading income and as much again in fees and payments for contract work. There is a wide range of grants made available to the voluntary sector in the countryside as well as the inner cities. In relation to the Urban Programme, the DOE attaches significant importance to local authorities working with the voluntary sector. Schemes which mobilise the resources of the communities themselves and projects which benefit disadvantaged minorities are encouraged. Under the Special Grants Programme, the Department makes grants to the central administrative costs of national organisations working in any of its fields of interest. It has a separate programme for grants or loans to voluntary organisations concerned with homelessness, including housing advice projects. There are also other projects whereby the voluntary sector may receive support (for EC funding for voluntary organisations see Department of Employment 1988: 123).

Even so, in a press release dated 10 July 1989 the NCVO said that government inefficiency was stifling voluntary action. Government was accused of a lack of clarity about the grant giving process, poor communications, inconsistency (a single voluntary agency can be pulled in different ways by different departments whose co-ordination *inter se* was claimed to be minimal) and so on.

The Players and the Author

To lead us into our next section, it will be useful to conclude on the relationship between the myriad of actors and players involved in the field of ICR and the existence, or otherwise, of a game-plan to mix metaphors rather vigorously. Is there, in other words, a single hand at work directing all these activities or not? Is there any real coherence emerging out of this flurry of activity? There are numerous experiments on offer and models are beginning to emerge which might be developed.

For example, the call for co-ordinating regional agencies has found expression in a number of different ways. The region-wide version of the local enterprise board, recently adopted by the West Midlands and the West Yorkshire boards, which now cover the whole of their respective regions rather than just the main conurbations, is one interesting development (Martin 1989: 47). The Welsh Development Agency, established in 1976, has also been frequently remarked upon for the great strides it has taken in attracting industry to the Principality. The WDA is partly financed by the Secretary of State and by borrowing from the National Loans Fund, the ECSC and the European Investment Bank. It has three wholly-owned subsidiaries which undertake investment in venture capital projects. Its Board is largely employer dominated but there is trade union involvement and, as is typical in Wales, informal contact with a wide range of groups is constantly practised. In 1988/9 new records were set in inward investment, business counselling services and land reclamation. It plays a leading role as property developer and landlord but also encourages others to come forward and identify and exploit opportunities for future development. Joint ventures and partnerships have a high priority for the WDA which is currently working closely with private developers, local authorities and other public sector bodies (WDA 1989). The success of the WDA is widely acclaimed, even if there are those who claim that it has received favourable treatment. Be that as it may, the record of achievement in the field of regeneration in recent years is highly impressive given the scale of the problem faced and the global resources available.

The Scottish Development Agency, established in 1975 is, of course, the tartan counterpart and again has received high praise for its endeavours. It does, however, seem to have been subject to strong ideological vicissitudes according to some commentators. From originally being a flagship of traditional state intervention in a troubled economy it appears to have gone through several distinct phases, culminating in what has been termed, post-1985, the 'self-help' model (Boyle 1988). Whatever the position adopted, the SDA has been able to do more than would have been possible where no large single agency had been in place. Any failures in policy-adoption and direction probably says more about the absence of an effective regional politics than anything else. The new status of the SDA as part of Scottish Enterprise will be watched with some interest.

English experience with such bodies is somewhat more limited. The Northern Development Company (NDC) is the most important example. It was formed in 1987 out of the ashes of the North Eastern Development Council which was almost entirely concerned with overseas inward investment. The NDC asked for a broader brief including regional development directed to supporting and expanding indigenous industry. It is a company limited by guarantee with an independent chairman, industrialists, local councillors, trade unionists and others on the board. It is also registered as an enterprise agency. Almost two-thirds of its budget comes from the Invest in Britain Bureau (which is a branch of the DTI) while the local authorities provide most of the rest of the funding, though there is a little private sector and trade union money as well. At the outset the DTI provided core funding of some £200,000, though that has now ceased. The NDC also attracts a large number of secondments.

What is distinctive is that it is the only Development Company in England to have a regional development remit, albeit that that is a very small part of its work compared to the inward investment side (NDC 1990). It is, nevertheless, obviously a body with great potential if there were clear government support for regional activity. The NDC is not much involved with the Urban Programme, though it will usually see the applications and comment upon them, but spends some time trying to bring industry together to make bids for money from various sources. In this way, it seems to be more active than BIC in the region. It is also closely involved with the Newcastle CAT which sometimes funds its projects. It has also recently put together a Northern Property Group funded by the private sector which has a number of interesting features, including providing a properties data-base and acting as a marketing device for particular sites. It has set up an economic research office, been a founder member of the Northern Media Forum, been involved in sector working groups, is in the process of producing a business survey for the Newcastle TEC and produces a quarterly economic review for the North of England (*Business Review North*). Even so, the feeling remains that there is no game plan for the region while central government still holds the whip hand, as for instance in establishing the UDC which was almost certainly not the preferred solution in the region. My feeling after discussions with the NDC and other actors in the area is that regional development capital was thought to be crucial and that if matching funds could be promised then partnership developments would be much enhanced. It is, some would think, a pity that central government is not extending the role of the NDC and is no longer, apparently, considering replicating its development functions in other areas. Other regional development organisations have, apparently, looked at the possibilities of undertaking programmes similar to those of the NDC yet, according to the DTI, none have put programmes or firm proposals for programmes together. I was informed by the DTI that 'Requests for such funding would of course be considered on their merits and against competing claims for resources'. The lack of enthusiasm for such an idea, with its longer-term implications for some level of regional autonomy, shines through the diplomatic language of the response. Compare this with the views of a House of Lords Committee:

> We recommend that the activities of the Development Agencies should be taken as a model for exploiting more effectively the technological and industrial potential of other areas of the United Kingdom, building on local loyalties and existing organisations. They should emulate the example of the Länder in Germany, which take a strategic view of technological and industrial development and support a broad range of activities which encourage innovative manufacturing industry. (Select Committee on Science and Technology 1991: 39)

This has perhaps been something of a mish-mash; a run around some, but by no means all, the actors involved in the field of inner city regeneration. At least the sheer proliferation of initiatives must dazzle the newcomer to this area and must raise the faint suspicion that more and more trees do not necessarily make a satisfactory wood. One commentator puts the case fairly strongly:

> The 1980s witnessed a mushrooming of organisations designed to promote development. However, it has become abundantly clear that an approach based on 'the more the better' is not the answer to Britain's economic problems. There is concern that the weak overall structure of economic development means that lessons are not learned and we have to keep reinventing the wheel. Indeed, some claim that the structure is counter-productive - being complex, inefficient and fragmented by increasing competition between similar agencies. (Brunskill 1990: 26)

We have seen too that the Audit Commission has suggested that different agencies might well be pursuing different visions of the future of the areas in which they operate, always assuming that they have vision at all. My discussions with people in the field have also indicated that the market in agencies does make monitoring and audit extremely difficult. Lack of coherence and a plethora of agents is not merely a British phenomenon (Blakely 1989: 257-63), but a strong argument can be made that Britain has overdone experiments-in-living when it comes to the process of regenerating the inner cities.

Chapter Four
Some Lessons

The United Kingdom is perhaps notorious for muddling through, for reacting to events, for crisis management. Planning in any real sense seems to be anathema to our system of government. An elaborate democratic architecture is amongst the casualties of this cast of mind; thus the democratic deficit is everywhere to be seen (Lewis and Harden 1986). The experience so far of inner city regeneration illustrates this culture in a classical fashion. Let us begin with the lack of grand vision. Quite apart from the opinions of the Audit Commission, which have already been mentioned, other reservations have been expressed:

> There is at present insufficient information to assess
> the strategic impact of the various programmes and
> initiatives involved. (NAO 1990)

A constitutional lawyer of a rationalist disposition will have as his, in this case, main preoccupation, the rationality and the openness of the machinery and institutions available for securing national objectives. This one has long argued that there is a substantial convergence in institutional terms between efficient and effective policy-making and civic and constitutional expectations (Birkinshaw *et al* 1990: ch. 5). ICR in Britain displays extraordinary weaknesses in meeting those claims. Let me begin at the centre.

At least one Department of Government has gone public on the need for strategic co-ordination:

> If central government is to be an effective partner at
> the local level then it must have an effective
> mechanism for co-ordinating the delivery of its main
> programmes. (DOE 1990: 19)

We have seen, however, that some have argued that a clear political
lead and commitment from central government is lacking (AMA 1986).
Now, granted that much has changed since 1986 there is still no
co-ordinated approach either at the Cabinet or at the Parliamentary
level. Indeed, the two Departments with main responsibility for ICR
have found it notoriously difficult to work together in total harmony.
After the 1988 high profile exercise, the Chancellor of the Duchy of
Lancaster was given responsibility for co-ordinating the inner city
programme and even had a small staff in the Cabinet Office. The
following year responsibility was transferred to the DOE in general
terms and now no Cabinet Minister has an ICR portfolio as such. We
have seen that the DTI currently does not actively support regional
enterprise bodies and there is little sign that Whitehall intends to
devolve policy and finance to the regions in the way that many regard
as necessary. Indeed, even the monitoring and review capacities of
central government have been heavily criticised from time to time. We
have seen that the NAO considered in 1990 that there should be a more
systematic review of achievements by the DOE and that, in the past,
the monitoring of urban development grants has relied heavily on local
authorities. The DOE does evaluate particular projects in which it has,
especially, an experimental interest, as in the case of Cruddas Park.
Yet, it must be remembered that only a short time ago the European
Commission was commenting adversely on the monitoring of the
European Structural Funds by the British Government (House of
Lords 1988). The Audit Commission has made it clear that monitoring,
review and assessment needs to be conducted both on the project level
and at the strategic level, a matter taken for granted in the United
States (Blakely 1989: 247-9). It should also be said that the Audit
Commission is now satisfied that the DOE has put in place a
comprehensive monitoring system of different inner city programmes
(Audit Commission 1989: 15).

However, the main institutional response of government has
been to put in place CATs and Task Forces in a number of inner city
areas. CATs are inter-departmental teams which focus on
co-ordination between different programmes. Each team comprises
the regional directors of the Departments of the Environment,
Employment, and Trade and Industry, together with a small
secretariat. They target their efforts on the needs of the inner city and

encourage private sector action and involvement. In spite of their clear successes they have been subject to criticisms by the Audit Commission, many of which have been responded to positively. Even so, as we have seen, they are limited in number and the sums available to them are such that they are likely to concentrate on specific projects at the expense of a wider co-ordinating role.

Task Forces, on the other hand, are small groups of secondees from the civil service, private sector, local government and voluntary bodies based in local offices and designed to find local solutions to local problems. Initially established by the DOE in eight inner city areas they are now the responsibility of the DTI. The NAO found that they had been well managed and monitored, and successful in their small areas. Yet increasingly heavy workloads are making it difficult for them to stimulate or help other organisations to contribute to the regeneration process. The DTI has now placed a higher priority on the need to strengthen the capacity of local organisations. More resources would enable more to be done, yet of course they are seen to be task-oriented, short-life institutions (NAO 1990: 14).

The CATs have been successful in their own way, yet even their members have remarked that their tasks could be done by other means or other agencies. Indeed, in some cases they have been. In fact, the CATs of themselves do not necessarily produce 'regeneration forums' of the various interest groups. Indeed, where such forums exist they appear to do so independently of government influence. Furthermore, it appears to be fortuitous as to whether even sectoral arrangements exist in the inner cities. Sector working parties have been active, for instance, in the Tyne and Wear region over the years covering, *inter alia*, clothing and IT software, with varying degrees of success. This means, in reality, that forums exist at the sectoral, or *meso* level, but not, so to speak at the city or regional 'macro' level. Sectors of industry may therefore be organised whether at the level of the city or the region. However, it is rare for cities (*a fortiori* regions) to establish forums which relate to a total economic plan or vision. In Newcastle at least they have used the CAT/DTI secretariat, though the impetus has been largely through the Northern Development Company. Currently the DTI seems not to favour such arrangements, preferring instead either short-life Task Forces or for the job to be taken over by trade associations. There is, it appears, once more a certain amount of ideological motivation at work in rejecting arrangements which might be thought by outsiders to be more rational. What perhaps swims against the tide of government thinking in this respect is Scottish Enterprise, which appears to be organised in sectoral fashion (see p. 57).

A few individual cities have made remarkable strides both in terms of promoting growth and development, and of creating working partnerships with most of the important actors. Some have managed to do so with reference to their structure or unitary development plans. A word or two about these at the outset. These development plans are intended to map out the *general* use to which land in the relevant area should be put in the medium term; they are not conclusive as to land-use development applications but act only as guidance. Their future has been somewhat uncertain over the last decade but they have been refined and reissued in Wales, which has given added focus to the development of South Glamorgan and brought Cardiff Bay into the account. The system of unitary plans for the metropolitan authorities is of particular interest. Although criticised for not taking in a larger geographical area, they have, most notably in Birmingham, sought to unite their statutory responsibilities with plans for economic development in the areas. Birmingham has done so with a degree of consultation which has won wide approval. The Audit Commission and the DOE have now also approved the practice.

A further word on development plans is called for in relation to UDCs. The DOE has decided that local authorities should not draw up unitary development plans (UDPs) for UDC areas, but rather that unitary development plans should adopt the strategies of the UDCs. Moreover, local authorities are required to take into account in their unitary development plans the impact of UDCs outside the UDC's area. In effect then, UDCs become the plan-making authorities for their areas - and have the right to influence planning matters well outside their areas. This is a major step beyond the powers of UDCs set out in the Local Government Planning and Land Act 1980 (CLES 1990: 41). The point worth making is that for every two steps forward towards rational planning in the area of ICR there seems to be an attendant one step backward.

Birmingham has also been in the forefront of authorities which has sought to bring together a forum of interested parties to plan the development of the city. The celebrated 'Highbury Initiative' deserves particular reference. This produced a symposium sponsored by the City Council and the Birmingham CAT which sought to review progress in revitalising the City Centre, to improve implementation and communication with all the interests concerned, to engage the local business community in the process and to build a sense of partnership. It resulted in a proposal to create a City Centre Forum directed in part to ensuring that the public and private sectors could work effectively together. As of writing the City Forum had not developed as such though there are numerous partnerships for particular development sites. What is significant, however, is the partnership between the City and the financial community in the form of 'City 2000' which has its own salaried chief executive   The local authority is, naturally, represented on the Board. At the moment, then, Birmingham operates through project or sector forums rather than on the global level, although an Economic Development Forum is expected to come into existence in late 1991. In any event, exciting developments have occurred in a much more patterned way than has often been the case elsewhere (Birmingham Heartlands 1989, Birmingham City Council 1989).

Sheffield is another example of a city which has spent considerable pains and energies in planning the development of the area, in spite of the poor press it has received over the staging of the World Student Games in 1991 and its previously poor set of relations with industry and commerce. It was one of the first large cities in Britain to establish a forum which had institutional continuity. The forum was Sheffield Economic Regeneration Committee (SERC), established in 1986, which was promoted by the City Council at the outset as a loosely organised body which used, as its main focus, a report commissioned from Coopers and Lybrand. It was immediately published and identified a number of flagship projects as well as outlining the strengths and weaknesses of the sub-region. SERC contains membership from business, commerce, local government, the higher education sector, central government and so on. It also has sub-groups concerned with social and community development, training and the like. There is representation from the TEC and the UDC so that as much common purpose is created as is possible in such circumstances. SERC has now promoted *Sheffield 2000* which is set to carry the city forward beyond the World Student Games. At a SERC meeting in 1989 a framework and timetable was developed to co-ordinate a number of long-term strategic plans for the city. These included the Unitary Development Plan, the SDC's strategy and the like. An organisational structure was established to develop and sustain it. A working party sought opinions and ideas about current initiatives before seeking to define the strategy. This included organising workshops, consulting business and community organisations and mounting an exhibition. It remains to be seen how far such good intentions bear fruit. However, there is little doubt in my mind that a forum of all interests with a strong communitarian commitment can only improve the rationality and effectiveness of regeneration policies.

Partnerships of various sorts are of the essence. Business and government must clearly work together, but there is little doubt that government should take the lead. The early failure of Universiade in Sheffield may be seen as the failure of an 'equal' partnership with no-one in the driving seat. Clearly local government, as the elected body, must have ultimate responsibility but it needs encouragement from the centre. The questions reduce themselves to two; what is the appropriate level of territorial government to take effective decisions in this area and will central government give them a sufficient degree of encouragement and autonomy to carry out the necessary decisions?

From time to time Boston, Massachusetts, has been mentioned. One final word may be useful at this point. While it is abundantly clear that Boston can plan growth in a way denied to all but a handful of cities around the world, it has, nevertheless, produced a series of initiatives and styles to which others might usefully pay close attention. The Boston Redevelopment Agency (BRA) has a broad range of powers which allows it to be the commanding force in terms of development projects in the city. It has developed an extensive range of institutions designed to ensure that developers take on board a wide range of community concerns and, for the most part, holds competitions for developers which require formalised consultation with the groups concerned. To some limited extent, both the Tyne and Wear Development Corporations and the Welsh Development Agency have been attempting to follow these patterns (For 'Community Monitoring Panels' see Tyne and Wear Development Corporation 1990, WDA 1990 for 'Property Development Opportunities'). Boston normally requires competition for its prime development opportunities, the criteria including environmental, social and community considerations as well as straightforward commercial ones. A draft Environmental Impact Report is made presenting the environmental and socio-economic consequences associated with the implementation of each alternative. Following its submission and review by the community, a preferred alternative will be selected with full knowledge of the environmental impact and other considerations. In recent years the BRA selected Columbia Plaza Associates to serve as the minority partner for a major development in the city. It was a partnership of Asian-American, black and Hispanic entrepreneurs. The Parcel 19 Task Force involved the Chinese communities in partnership with the BRA to develop a community package and 'linkage' arrangements for another development. Community benefits plans almost invariably accompany the selection process. It should be said too that Cardiff Bay, in its regeneration strategy, proposed a series of development briefs which go some considerable way towards the Boston practice.

Boston is, of course, something of a special case but communitarian politics run deep in the city while public and administrative law requirements at both the Federal and State levels seeks to ensure both greater rationality and participation than is often the case in Britain. The Audit Commission, perhaps unknowingly, underwrites much American practice in arguing for a proper economic development strategy to be adopted which involves a broad range of organisations within the community. They argue for a corporate approach, consistency between the various batches of planning documents and effective procedures for monitoring and review (Audit Commission 1989: 8). It is worth saying at this juncture that such aspirations only make sense in a culture of greater openness than is frequently the case in Britain. Above all, the local dimension has to be reinforced:

> Local decision-making and local control of resources
> for innovation and other production factors are
> therefore essential if areas are to respond to diverse
> and rapidly changing circumstances. (Brunskill 1990:
> 16)

A new favourite device for this purpose is the regeneration and/or social audit. The Audit Commission has done valuable work in recommending a review of the local economy which assesses its strengths and weaknesses and the opportunities and threats affecting it leading to decisions on action. The Commission made no recommendation about leadership of the audit, provided it was unambiguous but strongly urged that central government should set a national framework. In fact the DOE has been heavily involved in piloting such audits which the Commission recommends should operate in five stages (Audit Commission 1989: 50). What they were very clear about was that reviews should take place across normal institutional boundaries; for example, a review of land allocations would involve both the local authority and the DOE but also the private sector so that scope for identifying improved use of public sector land holdings might be identified. Publication of interim findings and proposals was urged and central government was encouraged to be more strategically minded and less project minded than in the past. A code of good practice in the form of an Audit Guide has also now been made available

What appears implicit in the approach of the Audit Commission is both a greater degree of openness in institutional terms and in terms of detail than has been common and that a body charged with the responsibility *and the authority* to carry out the economic development process is required. The latter point is more significant than it might appear since it brings us back both to the issue of relative autonomy and the scope to fulfil its role. This particular point reopens the issue of the optimum physical and social size of the area to be the subject of strategic planning.

We have looked at some of the more interesting experiments: the WDA, more recently The Wearside Opportunity in the North-East, the NDC and the SDA. We have also seen some of their shortcomings; to which may be added the occasional disagreements which arise between the WDA and the local authorities on the siting of plants, which may also say something about the absence of effective regional planning even within an area as small as Wales. But the new Scottish Enterprise (SE) will repay further study once it has had time to establish itself. It came into being just as this essay was going to press so that no assessment on the merits is possible. Even so, its frame and terms of reference merit attention. It is, in effect, a product of the merger of the SDA and the Training Agency in Scotland. For present purposes I shall ignore Highlands and Islands Enterprise. Having achieved the organisational merger of enterprise and training, it then seemed appropriate to split the organisation operationally to create a degree of decentralisation of effort to a network of thirteen local enterprise councils, responsible for eighty three per cent of the combined budget. What is immediately interesting is that the local enterprise councils have a certain degree of economic development power as well as responsibility for training and related matters. There is more of an accent on business development at first sight than exists for the TECs in England and Wales, Thus, for instance Lanarkshire Development *(sic)* Agency's 'mission statement' speaks of 'focusing public investment in the region'. Lothian and Edinburgh, unsurprisingly perhaps, will be concerned with developing the region's tourism and business visitor markets while Glasgow Development Agency refers to the need for bringing derelict land back into use. The other point of interest, already referred to, is that SE operates in divisions approximating to sectoral responsibilities (*Insider* 1991).

Scotland has often been treated differently from the rest of Britain and it may be that no grand design is at work; that this is not the ICR equivalent of the poll tax. Even so, in providing two regional bodies responsible for economic development in Scotland, structured in this particular way, we may be observing the beginnings of some strategic rationality in the process of being worked out. Money, of course, is crucial and SE is already complaining that it is beginning its life in straitened times given the reduction of the training budget announced by the DE in late 1990. All manner of suggestions have emerged for bankrolling local development (for example, Association of District Councils 1983), none of which has so far found general favour. Indeed, there is some dissatisfaction at the way in which Britain responds to EC funding for the regions where the Community has effectively redrawn the policy map. There currently appears to be no economic strategy at either a national or a regional level to which EC funding can clearly relate. The Community now requires regions to submit community economic development programmes spanning a period of three years in order to qualify for EC funding.

Brunskill is not the only one to argue for regional funding according to needs-based criteria to meet the problems of regeneration. She suggests several models of which the elected one is her preference. Nevertheless she envisages the possible alternative of a 'public interest company'. In either event the bodies would develop their own policies within guidelines set by government. An inter-departmental central government body should set guidelines, and allocate resources to the regions which would then plan, dispense and receive applications for funding from more local levels (Brunskill 1990).

Continuing and more effective evaluation of ICR is called for from the centre of government. Perhaps the effect of the 1989 Housing and Local Government Act and the new policy documents will advance this process. One can but hope. However, it seems clear that government over recent years has placed too much faith in the ability of market forces to solve problems and has failed to match the complex and interlocking nature of the problems found in urban areas with a co-ordinated inter-departmental and inter-agency response. There is clearly also need for longer-term commitments, especially regarding infrastructure and the environment. Once more, the 'lego'-like constitution of the UK seems unable to meet new challenges effectively, only to score random successes and then seek to improve the efficiency count of the score so far achieved:

> A failure in policy integration prevents us from grasping that an exceedingly complex urban problem is compounded by the fact that government departments which make policy, like the social sciences themselves, are subdivided into discrete specialisations (housing, transport, employment), while the life experience of cities in poverty is holistic.
> (Carley 1990)

Chapter Five
Conclusions

The British State is highly centralised, highly networked, and does not traditionally regard law as the great interpreter of the pattern of politics (Dyson 1980: 41). A great deal has changed in recent years; we have entered Europe, we have engaged in a huge programme of privatisation, we have given tremendous rhetorical and financial support to reinvigorated markets; we are even about to hive off some eighty or more per cent of the civil service into semi-autonomous agencies that are much more distanced from Parliament than formerly. All this has been done with the minimum of constitutional engineering and without any great national debate. Progress towards inner city regeneration has to be seen in that light. The cities deteriorated without national heartsearching in the first place and they are being patched up without a national strategy. Even so, enormous changes have been at work in this area in circumstances where constitutional forms of accountability have played little or no part and where democratic traditions have played their part only where determination has been shown at the local level.

The absence of an articulate system of public law is as much evident in terms of ICR as elsewhere; no open and authoritative design process, no patterned legal duties of consultation, no FOI (except in the beleaguered town halls); not even a set of enforceable complaints procedures save the intermittent sallies of the unlinked ombudsman systems. Local authority power has diminished while the role of business has been elevated, from time to time, as a form of alternative legitimation for what has been and ought to be achieved. But there can be no dispute; for all the vital interventions of local government, industry and the voluntary and community sectors, the power of central government has been strengthened. It has been a central apparatus that only reluctantly embraces planning, design and strategic responsibility. Instead it has come to ask local government to assume strategic responsibilities without being afforded the power. Local authorities have had to come to terms with business, with central government, with UDCs, with TECs, and with a multitude of changes in institutional forms in the knowledge that if they did not express belief in their local communities, few others would.

The result has been a record of considerable achievement and considerable disappointments. The process of ICR has been underfunded, the funding has been unbalanced, rarely strategically rational, and too little autonomy has been delegated to those who have the interest and the expertise to do what is necessary. Indeed, we may still be at the stage where in response to 'what is the answer to ICR' we may still need to ask 'what is the question'? This is not as quirky as it sounds. Are we seeking to reduce unemployment in some areas at the expense of others? Are we intent on removing blips and blind spots? Are we, like the Germans, committed to a game of economic equilibrium between the regions? Are we committed to market freedoms with only the worst externalities attended? Or what? Even seemingly anodyne remarks may not be entirely unproblematical as when Scottish Enterprise sees its overall objective as being that of 'assisting the market to work more effectively ... while seeking to remedy market failure and distortion' (*Scottish Enterprise* 1991). Failure to do what and distorting what are very much political questions so that they need to be posed clearly at the political level and also at the 'right' or 'optimum' political level. Just as there is dispute over 'subsidiarity' in the European Community so there is heated debate over the shape and powers of territorial government in Britain, as elsewhere. What an examination of the recent record of ICR makes clear is that we have not yet adequately addressed these issues in Britain and that until we do, it is less than fruitful to talk about the efficiency and the effectiveness of different policies.

Government in Britain is rarely conducted in the sunlight. It is not, however, always undercover; rather it is *Government by Moonlight* (Birkinshaw *et al* 1990). ICR again proves the point. Local government must consult and publish under the 1989 Act where it is engaged in economic development. Central government is often coy about its intentions and its thinking and is not subject to the FOI equivalents of local government under the Local Government (Access to Information Act) 1985. Nor, interestingly, are the UDCs, yet some of them are extremely keen to operate openly and occasionally, as in Tyne and Wear, will choose developers for sites after a keen competition which involves seeking public views on the preferred developer (Tyne and Wear Development Corporation 1989). There is little doubt that good practices can be found across the spectrum of development in our inner cities and equally that poor practice and failure to communicate are readily detectable. It is the failure to be rational, open, clear, committed and accountable that is so evident in most aspects of our system of governance. ICR bears this out once more with a ringing clarity.

We have seen that the Audit Commission has commented favourably upon the improvements put in place by the DOE, both in relation to improved monitoring and in terms of its willingness to assess the impact of different schemes. Even so, the question must remain as to whether the Government is constitutionally rational enough to provide the means of achieving what are no doubt desired ends. There is also the inescapable fact that, at present, central government appears not to trust local government. It cannot, on the one hand, encourage it to be the promoter of economic development while appearing to argue that local government is not a suitable body to organise schooling within its area, except at the most generalistic level. This may be especially so given the traditional hostility of governments of the right and of business to what is usually seen as bureaucratic meddling in economic affairs. An acceptance of the constitutional rights of territorial government and the adjustment of its legitimate relations with the business community seems to me to be a pre-requisite of real progress in this area. All efforts to identify and encourage the use of codes of good practice cannot disguise this basic fact. The following statement from a private sector secondee to the DOE perhaps summarises the problem:

> The present government has concentrated on an economic/enterprise-led approach to urban regeneration as opposed to environment/social improvements. The reason is that only improving job opportunities and skills will people acquire independence. Any other approach locks them into dependency and may, indeed self-evidently has in this country in earlier years and in some other countries, end up by worsening their condition. (Charleston 1989)

This view is still too common for the observer to admit of a renewed respect for local government. Indeed, one of the clearest messages coming from those involved in ICR at the local authority level is that the rhetoric from government is never wholeheartedly enthusiastic about what can be achieved, so that signals to private industry about the competence and utility of local authority help and assistance are not wholeheartedly made. Even Birmingham, which has been so conspicuously successful in regenerating its local economy in recent years, and whose relations with the DOE have usually been good, has felt thwarted in relation to some of its major developments, not least the National Exhibition Centre. The delegated powers to the Secretary of State under the 1989 Act have not yet been finalised, but the feeling is that restraints on borrowing as part of the general concern with the PSBR has already inhibited the Council from acting in what it sees as the long-term interests of the City.

The lack of rationality of the whole process, intimately connected with the constitutional apparatus of British government, has already been argued. Even so, another major issue has to be raised. It refers to the socio-economic inequalities between the regions, which appear, many would argue, to have widened in recent years:

> In practice, the Conservative's Government (*sic*)
> programme for restructuring the economies of the
> regions was almost certain to be socially and spatially
> divisive. (Martin 1989: 47)

ICR and the EC

The European dimension also needs to be addressed. The Structural Funds are, of course, to be doubled by 1993 and some forty per cent of the Community's population living in areas of industrial decline are in Britain. Some have argued that the EC has effectively redrawn the regional policy map of Britain and obliged the various Government Departments to work together in drawing up regional programmes which are increasingly of the integrated development operation type so effectively turned to advantage by the City of Birmingham (Birmingham City Council 1990, Audit Commission 1991). As the Audit Commission has pointed out, preparation of the new Operational Programmes has required the setting up of *ad hoc* regional groupings to prepare and implement the programmes.

There is differential experience of the success of the partnerships between central and local government in terms of access to European Funds. It is common for regional government offices to act as the secretariat for bids by local authorities and in many cases they do so very effectively. However, much seems to depend on the Department concerned, on the region, and, of course, on how effectively regional groupings can cohere and present a united front. In any event, most programmes are still locally prepared and local authorities are expected to take the lead in assembling programmes and drawing in other bodies as appropriate. Since these bids are competitive and not quota-based, the need for an integrated approach is made manifest. I have already referred to the Sheffield 2000 initiative, but to capitalise on the availability of European funding a conference organised by the South Yorkshire Local Authorities in April 1990 produced a report, *South Yorkshire 2000*, which is an attempt to provide an integrated regional approach to common problems in part via the EC. Nor is this development unique since there also exists, for instance, a West Midlands Regional Forum which began life as a lobbying group for assisted area status and then to approach the EC for assistance in relation to regional transport needs. Again, we see territorial government taking the initiative. What constitutes a problem according to some, however, is that the absence of truly representative regional authorities makes it difficult for the local authority associations to contest some of central government's priorities for economic regeneration in the councils of Europe.

However we look at it, Britain has yet to produce a satisfactory response to the problem of regional assistance at the European level which satisfies the imperatives of the EC itself. One such is to provide:

> the foundation for decentralised management of
> assistance from the funds and for a genuine
> partnership at local, regional and national level ...
> assistance should be planned and provided in an
> efficient and unbureaucratic a manner as possible.
> (Bachtler 1990: 17)

At the time of writing Brussels had just announced that it was blocking £100 million aid to the UK under the 'Rechar' programme which is aimed at regenerating former mining areas. The UK's administration of funds had found disfavour within the Commission, not least on the grounds of lack of 'transparency', not, one must agree, the UK constitution's most obvious strength (*Financial Times* 29 April 1991).

The trends in European Community regional policy imply an increasing transfer of responsibility and decision-making power away from the national government level, to the Commission, in particular, but also to the regions. As Bachtler inquires; how far are national governments, and by implication, the British in particular, prepared to see this progressive transfer go and what are the implications?

The Resurgence of Territorial Politics?

It is not difficult to imagine a framework which would better suit a rational system of regionally-based regeneration, and intelligent ideas abound. The political will is another matter. However, let me return to Bachtler who encapsulates the issues at stake nicely. He argues for a national framework which would set the parameters for regional and local development which would create a framework of priorities and guidelines, not least to exercise some control to avoid competitive outbidding. It is interesting in this respect that the Welsh Development Agency and the local authorities in Wales have frequently come into conflict about the siting of major inward developments. Paramount, needless to say, would be a system for the distribution of regional financial resources. The second aspect of the strategy would involve regional and local implementation within the national framework. This regional layer would produce an 'autodiagnosis' exploiting the potential of the region, having conducted a regional audit which would include development opportunities. Finally, and I shall have a little more to say about this, a bottom-up decentralised range of sites would be encouraged to respond to local needs and harness local resources and knowledge in kilter with strategic authorities.

This policy structure involving the 'top-down' establishment of a framework, and 'bottom-up' implementation would involve:

> all relevant participants in both the public and private
> sectors... However, in emphasising the decentralised
> mode of implementation, the limits of its
> effectiveness will also have to be appreciated. The
> crucial determinant will inevitably be central
> government's approach to macro-economic
> management, overall industrial policy and social and
> infrastructure spending. The encouragement of
> local/indigenous potential is of little relevance in
> isolation, and factors such as the education and
> qualifications of the workforce, demographic
> characteristics, natural resources and industrial
> patterns are of fundamental importance. (Bachtler
> 1990: 17)

The integration of other programmes, such as TECs, would need to occur within such a framework for it to be effective, but it needs also to be stressed that the local level has a great deal to contribute (see also Goldsmith (1988: 31) for decentralisation experiences in much of Europe). Operating units need to be located near their target market to ensure that local issues and needs are incorporated within the terms of reference of the larger entity, flexibility is essential and the line of approval for projects must be kept as short as possible. Even so, with regional development agencies, involving all the major partners, being responsible to a regional tier of government the beginnings of strategically sensitive regeneration policies would be in sight (Martin 1989: 47).

Proposals such as these would fit easily into the expectations of the EC but the battle for revised territorial politics of this order has yet to be won in Britain. As and when reform takes place it is to be hoped that the opportunity will be taken to inject a strong public law element into the proceedings in order to prevent the kidnapping of a devolved system of government by the central authorities. A revised administrative and constitutional law could do much to improve the rationality of the regeneration process by developing institutions for visible corporate planning and monitoring procedures, for ensuring that adequate consultation occurred and to afford legal rights for objections to the overriding of local interests and concerns.

Although finance has been continually stressed, its source, some would argue, is less important than the uses to which it can be put. The following summarises this point of view:

> The issue is less how local and regional government
> raises money; many countries in Europe give fewer
> revenue raising powers to local government, even
> after the poll tax, than in Britain. Rather, the issue is
> how much competence, autonomy and discretion the
> centre permits the localities. (*Guardian* 13 June 1990)

This is also the view taken by some of those whom I have spoken to who are heavily involved in economic development in the inner cities. Regionalism raises ambivalent responses from some local actors, but they all stress that what really matters is whether they have real power and can operate without continued red-tape and second-guessing. The degree to which European government has become decentralised is scarcely recognised in the United Kingdom. In most other European countries, education, urban regeneration, industrial policy, even water and energy supplies are within the competence of local and regional government. Britain's recent constitutional mix is truly that of 'undemocratic centralism and neo-corporatism' (Lewis 1990). The response to change is simply inadequate. This summary from the economics page of the same issue of *The Guardian* newspaper again strikes an important note:

> This is an era where products need to be more
> customised and production more specialised and

> flexible. The manufacture of vast numbers of
> standard products is giving ground before both the
> demands of more discerning, richer final consumers
> and the installation of new key technologies
> throughout the economy.

The shock-waves are being felt not only in consumer industries, but the intermediate and capital goods industries that supply them. Government has to be more responsive to the quirks of the local industrial structure. It can no longer set standard rules and spending limits at the centre and expect them either to work or to be observed.

Local needs ought therefore to be accomodated in relation to the skills of the local workforce, the research programmes of numerous institutes, the shape of transport infra-structures and so on. The less responsive central government is to these local needs, according to this view, the less robust the immediate economy. This argument is so important to the ICR debate that it deserves an extended treatment.

There is, the argument goes, much to be said for a situation where political competence to launch a policy initiative at the local level exists, even if finance has then to be negotiated from the centre. This does not necessitate an abandonment of sound finance; merely a recognition that public sector investment need be no more inflationary than any other form of investment. Rotterdam is the example which is highlighted. Rotterdam receives nearly all its income from the central government rather than local taxes but as an independent city authority it has succeeded in developing its own docklands through a private-public partnership and not via a central government agency bypassing local government representatives as in London's Docklands. It is claimed that the result is a development more respectful of local economic needs and whose transport infrastructure has preceded the private development rather than following fitfully in its wake. The planning coordination is seen as pivotal. In order to deflect the 'one-swallow' barb, it is pointed out that the leaders in the European City League, on almost any set of indicators, are well-established masters of their political environment (*Guardian* 13 June 1990).

Differing views are, predictably, expressed by central government in Britain which is notoriously reluctant to embrace anything smacking of federal solutions when unbridled power at the centre can be so securely wielded by the few. Even so, and without wishing to close down any arguments, the lack of coordination of local economic initiatives in Britain must say something about our constitutional arrangements. Although I have welcomed much of the 1989 Act, especially in relation to the requirement to produce a strategic economic development statement, I might add on this point that none of the statements which I have so far seen have been produced after discussions with other local authorities in the region or sub-region.

Local Politics

At this point the local, community or neighbourhood level needs to be briefly readdressed. There is no doubt that over the years many local authorities have been unresponsive to the needs of their community; they have been distant, uncoordinated in their approach and unsympathetic. There is also considerable evidence that relations with their communities have improved in recent years, in no small measure due to their feeling the need to explain the cuts in services imposed on constituents by central government. This has been particularly evident in the field of ICR even though much remains to be done and even though liaison with local communities is fraught with difficulties, many of them related to the understandable apathy of the relatively disadvantaged. Nonetheless there are many clear advantages in local decision-making and local control of resources for innovation and delivery of services (Brunskill 1990: 16, 28).

There are many instances of drawing the local communities into the decision-making processes within British ICR experience even if little approximates to the success of the Bostonian model where numerous features conspire to make that possible; geography, economic opportunity, ethnic culture, political charisma and, not least, a tradition of administrative law which acts as a surrogate political process. I still believe that that tradition is capable of guiding us to produce better outcomes than is normally the case here. The establishment of a social regeneration group within the Sheffield 2000 initiative may well represent the kind of lead which needs to be taken (Sheffield City Council 1990). Yet the Cruddas Park Estate in Newcastle perhaps provides more food for thought than other experiments. I shall not rehearse the role of the on-site, independent, community worker, nor the many experiments in consultation and community enterprise. However, it is the lessons which may emerge that should occupy our attention. From this point of view I believe it is time for the idea of Community Councils to be dusted down from their 1960s origins and need to be given local authority support. They might well constitute an issue which authorities were instructed to consider in drawing up their Section 35 strategies under the 1989 Act. Such bodies should have a right to summon officers and members to their deliberations so that a truly two-way dialogue is encouraged. For their part, if such community bodies are to be resourced, they will need to be organised efficiently and to account for any use of resources entrusted to them. There is much to be said for area development teams within urban conurbations to liaise with local communities. There are many ways in which an Urban Ministry, whether the DOE or not, could address such issues but the communities need to feel that they have some leverage. The jurisdiction of the local ombudsman might also be re-examined with a view to seeing what contribution it could make to the enfranchisement of community groups.

Concluding Remarks

There is little doubt that there is a need to concentrate policy on the local economy in order to provide a base for self-sustaining growth. The movement of companies into poorer regions has never, of itself, occurred on a large enough scale to solve the problems at stake. The public sector must take a leading role in the development or regeneration policy, preferably through a reborn system of territorial politics in the regions. There is also compelling logic in bringing together the many strands involved in ICR through an Urban/Territorial Government Ministry with cabinet status. Whatever public/private partnerships are conceived, it is government which must take the lead and there is urgent need for a degree of local government autonomy in this and other areas. Private industry must be encouraged but it is clear that the decision by recent central government administrations to reduce dramatically their spending on regional policy has caused great hardship and has held back the development of the poorer areas. Whatever benefits are attached to market forces it is clear that market allocation and competitive forces are structured and moulded by the socio-economic and institutional frameworks within which they operate. These are largely made and unmade by government.

The logic of what has preceded is that funding for regional policy should be increased and paid directly to the regional bodies in the form of a block grant and allocated according to needs (and see Brunskill 1990: 34). Regional and sub-regional enterprise boards might well be the appropriate mechanisms for delivering on economic regeneration policies, especially where they were partnership forums, provided they are ultimately responsible to the appropriate tier of government. Renewed attention would have to be paid to the matter of regional venture capital funding. All this will prove possible once we ask who should control the public monies and who the regeneration is supposed to benefit.

I have been concerned to examine the rationality of the machinery and institutions available for securing, moving-target objectives in the area of inner city regeneration. My conclusions, in spite of notable achievements, are not entirely favourable. The failures of our constitutional machinery at large to assist in bringing about the conditions for national well-being and success are notorious and are replicated in the ICR field. I am forced to conclude once more that there is a potential convergence in institutional terms between efficient and effective policy-making and about civic and constitutional expectations. I believe in one sense that the post-Fordist, flexibilisation of bureaucracies offers real opportunities to augment the dignified parts of the constitution with new administrative régimes which can address themselves to consumer satisfaction and the enfranchisement of pluralistic communities.

There is a great deal of expertise and experience in many fields in the local authority arena and other public (and indeed voluntary) agencies. This needs to be put to full use. This approach is perhaps getting underway, but now needs planning on a more formal long-term basis. The planning frameworks for economic regeneration are inadequate. No organisations can be expected to progress without corporate planning and monitoring devices, including measurable performance indicators, both economic and social. There is still no evidence that cost benefit analysis techniques are being properly developed in the social and political field. As and when such devices are in place, learning requirements are such that the widest constituencies need to be involved, yet communitarian politics and the machinery for their promotion are inadequate in our inner cities.

Inner city regeneration policies in recent years have seen many successes and many failures. A great deal remains to be done. Here, as elsewhere, the architecture is all important. Constitutional principles require that constitutional actors be readily identified and that they should be readily called into account. Neither principle is currently being adequately invoked.

Bibliography

Association of District Councils (1983) *Economic Development by District Councils*, London, Association of District Councils.

Association of Metropolitan Authorities (1986) *Programme for Partnership: An Urban Policy Statement*, London, Association of Metropolitan Authorities.

Audit Commission (1989) *Urban Regeneration and Economic Development: The Local Government Dimension*, London, Audit Commission for England and Wales.

Audit Commission (1990) *Urban Regeneration and Economic Development Audit Guide*, London, Audit Commission for England and Wales.

Audit Commission (1991) *Urban Regeneration and Economic Development: The European Community Dimension*, London, Audit Commission for England and Wales..

Bachtler, J. (1990) *Issues in European Regional Development*, European Policies Research Centre, Glasgow.

Bennett, R., McCoshan, A., and Sellgren, J. (1989) *TECS and VET: The practical requirements: organisation, geography and international comparison with the USA and Germany*, Department of Geography, London School of Economics.

BIC (1987) *Neighbourhood Development Partnerships*, London, Business in the Community.

BIC (1988a) *The Future for Enterprise Agencies,* London, Business in the Community.

BIC (1988b) *Education Business Partnerships*, London, Business in the Community.

BIC (1989) *Companies in the Community; Guidelines for Company Boards*, London, Business in the Community.

BIC/BP (1987) *Business in the Inner Cities*, London, Business in the Community.

BIC and British Telecom (1988) *Handbook for Board Members of Local Enterprise Agencies*, London, Business in the Community.

Birmingham City Council (1989), *Birmingham Integrated Development Operation; First Report and Strategy Review*, Birmingham City Council.

Birmingham Heartlands (1989) Information pack; East Birmingham Inner City Renewal.

Birkinshaw, P., Harden, I., and Lewis, N., *Government By Moonlight, the Hybrid Parts of the State*, London, Unwin Hyman.

Blakely, E., (1989) *Planning Local Economic Development, Theory and Practice*, New York, Sage.

Boddy, M., (1988) 'Bristol: a study of economic change in the UK 'Sunbelt'', in Parkinson, M., Foley, B., and Judd, D., (eds) *Regenerating the Inner Cities, the UK crisis and the US experience*, Manchester University Press.

Boyle, R., (1988) 'Private sector urban regeneration: the Scottish Experience', in Parkinson, M., Foley, B., and Judd, D., (eds) *Regenerating the Inner Cities, the UK crisis and the US experience*, Manchester University Press.

British Rail (1988) *Cardiff Valleys Rail Development Strategy*, County of South Glamorgan, Mid Glamorgan County Council.

BRA, (1982) *Fact Book*, Boston Redevelopment Agency.

Brunskill, I., (1989) *The Regeneration Game, A Regional Approach to Regional Policy*, London, Institute for Public Policy Research.

Cabinet Office (1988) *Action for Cities*, London, Cabinet Office.

Cabinet Office (1989) *Progress on Cities*, London, HMSO.

Carley, M., (1990) *Housing and Neighbourhood Renewal: Britain's new urban challenge*, quoted in R. Freeson, 'Partnerships for Urban Renewal', *Search*, August 1990 Joseph Rowntree Foundation, York.

Cardiff Bay Development Corporation (1988) *Cardiff Bay Regeneration Strategy*, Cardiff Bay Development Corporation/ Llewelyn-Davies Planning.

Confederation of British Industry (1988) *Initiatives Beyond Charity:*

Report of the CBI Task Force on Business and Urban Regeneration, London, Confederation of British Industry.

Charleston, R., (1989) '*Private Sector Involvement in Urban Regeneration*', paper given at Civil Service College, October 1989.

CLES (1990) *Inner City Regeneration, A Local Authority Perspective, First Year Report of the CLES Monitoring Project on Urban Development Corporations*, Centre for Local Economic Strategies.

Cruddas Park (1989) *Feasibility Study into the Prospects of Social and Economic Regeneration in the Loadman Street and Cruddas Park Area of Newcastle*, Newcastle City Council.

Cruddas Park (1990) *Progress of a Project Tackling Inner City Regeneration, December 1988-90*, Cruddas Park Community Trust.

Department of Employment (1988) *Employment for the 1990s*, Cm 540, London, HMSO.

Department of Employment (1989) *Training and Enterprise Councils, A Second Industrial Revolution*, London, Department of Employment.

Department of Employment (1989) *Action For Cities, DOE Inner City Programmes*, London, Department of Employment.

Department of Employment (1990) *People in Cities*, London, HMSO.

Department of Trade and Industry (1989) *Reviving Inner Cities*, London, HMSO.

Department of Trade and Industry (1990) *The Enterprise Initiative*, London, DTI.

Dyson, K. (1980) *The State Tradition in Western Europe*, London, Martin Robertson.

Goldsmith, M., (1988), 'Social, economic and political trends and their impact on British Cities', in Parkinson, M., Foley, B., and Judd, D., (eds) *Regenerating the Inner Cities, the UK crisis and the US experience*, Manchester University Press.

House of Lords (1988) *Reform of the Structural Funds*, Select Committee on the European Communities, 14th Report, Session 1987-8, HL Paper 82.

Insider (1991), *Scottish Enterprise, An Integrated Network*, Special Report April 1991

Jenkins, K., Caines, K., and Jackson, A., (1988) *Improving Management in Government: the Next Steps; Report to the Prime Minister*, London, HMSO.

Judd, D. and Robertson, D. (1988) 'Urban revitalisation in the US: prisoner of the federal system', in Parkinson, M., Foley, B., and Judd, D., (eds) *Regenerating the Inner Cities, the UK crisis and the US experience*, Manchester University Press.

Lewis, N., (1989) 'A Standing Administrative Conference', *Political Quarterly*, 60, 421-432.

Lewis, N., (1990) 'Undemocratic Centralism and Neo-Corporatism: the New British Constitution', *Alberta Law Review*, 18, 540-553.

Lewis, N., (1991) 'Policy Styles: Trends, Cycles and the Missing Constitution', *Studies in Law*, Hull University Law School.

Lewis, N., and Harden, I., (1982) 'Law and the Local State', *Urban Law and Policy*, 5, 65-86.

Lewis, N., and Harden,I., (1986) *The Noble Lie: the British Constitution and the Rule of Law*, London, Hutchinson.

London Docklands Development Corporation (1989) *Corporate Plan 1989*, London Docklands Development Corporation.

London Docklands Development Corporation (1990) *Report and Accounts 1989-90* LDDC.

Martin, R., (1989) 'The New Economics and Politics of Regional Restructuring: the British Experience', in *Regional Policy at the Crossroads, European Perspectives*, Albrechts, L., Moulaert, F., Roberts, P., and Swyngedouw, E., (eds), London, Jessica Kingsley Publishers.

Merseyside Development Corporation (1989) *Annual Report and Financial Statements*, Liverpool, Merseyside Development Corporation.

National Audit Office (1990) *Regenerating the Inner Cities*, HC 169, London, HMSO.

NCVO (1988) *Releasing Enterprise, Voluntary Organisations and the Inner City*, London, National Council for Voluntary Organisations.

Newcastle City Council (1991) *Economic Activities 1991-2*, Development Committee.

Nicholson, F. (1989) 'Wearside - the Advanced Manufacturing Centre of the North', *Northern Executive*.

Northern Development Company (1990) *Annual Report*, Newcastle, Northern Development Company.

Public Accounts Committee (1989) *Urban Development Corporations*, 20th Report, Session 1988-9, HC 385, London, HMSO.

Select Committee on Science and Technology (1991), *Innovation in Manufacturing Industry*, 1st Report, Session 1990-91, HL 18-1, London, HMSO.

Sheffield City Council (1990) *Sheffield 2000, Phase One*, Sheffield City Council.

TUC (1988) *Trade Unions in the Cities*, London, Trades Union Council.
Tyne and Wear Development Corporation (1990) *Annual Report, Piloting Progress, Corporate Plan 1990-94*, Tyne and Wear Development Corporation.
Welsh Development Agency (1989) *Report and Accounts 1988/9*, Cardiff, Welsh Development Agency.
Welsh Development Agency (1990) Promotion Documents for Property Development Opportunities.